For James and Olive

# kelly doust
# the crafty minx

## creative recycling and handmade treasures

MURDOCH BOOKS

# Foreword

Hanging on a wall in my daughter's bedroom are two framed pieces of embroidery. Both are of old-fashioned scenes, with girls in pretty dresses set amongst a vibrant floral backdrop – simple and quaint, they are the perfect style of adornment for a young girl's room. Upon first gaze, it is clear that these are very special pieces, even treasures perhaps, not just because they are framed and hung, but because you can tell they are handmade. The slight irregularity of the edges gives it all away – a single imperfection that conveys the truth – that there were two hands behind their glorious creation. The fact that, in this case, the two hands belonged to my mother made them more special still.

Embroidered when she was a young girl of about ten, my mother kept them in a brown paper bag, buried deep in a cupboard at home. On occasion over the years, she would come across them by accident, gaze upon her handiwork and marvel at the idea that she could have created these thoughtful works at such a young age. I remember well watching on, as she would lose herself in the memory of each piece, recounting with a smile the circumstances around her making them. When eventually she passed them on to me, I knew that she was not merely passing on a keepsake; she was entrusting me with a piece of herself and of her life. And so, her creations live on – framed, hung and taking pride of place on the wall in my little girl's bedroom.

Generations before ours knew well that there is a kind of inner peace that comes to us when we are creating. A feeling so difficult to capture these days and yet so satisfying to the soul – where body, mind and spirit are working in rhythm. It's a quiet, meditative state of being; one which allows us to find clarity in the moment. Whether it is the creation of an artwork, the baking of a cake or embroidering of a cushion, we all have it in us to create of ourselves, for ourselves, in a way that brings us this peace and serenity.

Of course, it is one thing to want to create, it's another thing entirely to know where to begin. That's where Kelly Doust's *The Crafty Minx* is a saving grace – reconnecting a new generation with the lost art of craft making. Filled to the brim with inspired creations and ideas for all seasons, Kelly's luscious book is the ideal way to begin your creative journey. Perhaps your creations could become a keepsake – framed and adored upon a little girl's bedroom wall – or maybe in the process you may just find some room within for peace and tranquillity. Whatever the result – be confident in the knowledge that you are creating of yourself, for yourself. And if craft making can do that for you, then it's worth every stitch!

SHANNON FRICKE
Interiors expert, television presenter and
author of the *Sense of Style* series

# Contents

## autumn

## winter

## epilogue

# Embrace your inner Crafty Minx

*The Crafty Minx* is the story of my own discovery over the course of a year: that making and giving away handmade objects feeds the soul and, paired with recycling preloved or unwanted goods, provides immense satisfaction and karmic goodwill. In writing this book, I hope to share some simple skills and tips with you to prove just how easy it is to get creative with the unwanted objects in your life. By the end, you will be confident enough to undertake your own projects – even if you think you have zero talent as a seamstress.

Being a Crafty Minx is not about being perfect: it's about the vital importance of exercising your creative muscle to make stylish and clever crafts for yourself, your friends, your home and for, or with, children. You will make mistakes along the way, but that's okay: mistakes are human. Sometimes they are even charming.

◉◉◉

Even as a girl, I enjoyed making and reinventing things, but back then I had little patience for fiddling with sewing machines or patterns. I learned to sew when I was about seven or eight but far preferred five-minute projects with paper, scissors and glue. And shopping for fabric and trimmings. This was much to the chagrin of my grade nine home economics teacher, because although I had the boldest, prettiest dressing gown in the year to hand in as my final project, it was a testament to the gorgeous Japanese kimono fabric I had chosen, rather than the mess of wonky seams and loose threads that constituted my attempt to stitch it together.

## *The only true gift is a portion of thyself*

— RALPH WALDO EMERSON

As a teenager, I developed a passion for flea markets and charity shops and would often customise quality vintage finds so I could fit in with the latest fashions or make a statement at a party. When I say 'customise', I mean cutting a long frock into a mini dress ten minutes before I left the house and taking up the hem later on my trusty sewing machine. I was not averse to using a stapler in the interim.

Although initially spurred on by a budget and tendency to economise on clothes rather than going out or (later) feeding my French cheese and red wine addiction, when I finally found myself earning a higher income, I realised I actually preferred buying second-hand to brand new. These were once-beloved objects that had lived a life and had stories to tell! Mine was just a chapter in their existence, which somehow felt more meaningful (and glamorous) than owning new, but cheaply made products from China, which would fall apart in no time.

Wherever I was in the world, I would scour vintage and charity stores and markets searching for beautiful, unique items or fabrics I could buy for a song and fix up if need be. A kid in a candy store, I confess I sometimes treated my travels like one big shopping trip. Never very suited to the life of a backpacker, I sent my spoils back in stamp-covered boxes that I prayed would wend their way home. I hunted cashmere beaded cardigans and dusty linen Union Jack flags on Portobello Road in London and felt berets in 'Les Puces' (The Fleas) at Porte de Clignancourt in Paris, as well as '40s slips from hole-in-the-wall stores in New York's East Village, carpets in Istanbul's Grand Bazaar and traditional knotted shirts and finely-wrought silver filigree ornaments from hill tribes in

Northern Thailand. The fashion for wearing designer labels paraded on the outside of clothes never held much appeal.

Back home, I continued to track down the treasures in my local flea markets, charity and second-hand stores, but living in temporary accommodation meant I had to keep a strict 'one in, one out' policy.

When my husband and I bought our first home together recently, a Victorian 'Italianate' cottage (so called because of the stern plaster ladies who adorn the arch in our hallway like a pair of sphinxes), I started reinventing and making things in earnest, and not just to wear. After a nomadic life of flitting from share-house to share-house and country to country, our old/new home inspired me. I turned my hand to all sorts of things, from paintings and collages on canvas to fill the walls, to cosy lambswool throws and cashmere-covered cushions, made from old jumpers, for the sofa. I taught myself to renovate sombre, tired furniture with milk paint and beeswax, and even covered chairs and lampshades with luscious wallpaper and fabric remnants.

With our mortgage putting a dent in our disposable income, I rediscovered that necessity is indeed the mother of invention. I realised how intensely happy it made me to surround us with things I had made or reconditioned myself, and once again enjoyed a sense of history from my belongings. And as someone who suffers from a deficit of patience, I cut corners, kept things simple and they still turned out beautifully – most of the time.

I also found myself making gifts for friends and their children, which were received with an overwhelming amount of surprise and joy. I made clothes and soft toys for their new babies, homewares and accessories of all sorts for birthdays and Christmas presents, and handmade cards. I used their favourite colours or made something I knew they didn't have or could put to use, always making sure I had them in mind while I stitched or painted. I found out just how much people love receiving something unique, particularly when so few of us make things anymore. When time is a commodity we value most, spending it on someone you care about is unbelievably precious and will always be appreciated. And the best thing was, it often took me less time to make something than a trip to the shops would have. With a linen cupboard full of old jumpers I had handwashed, or materials that had caught my eye, as well as a minimal sewing kit, I had all the ingredients I needed for making great gifts anytime – even half an hour before I was due somewhere.

You may have gathered that (like most people) I love shopping. I also can't resist reading an avalanche of fashion and design magazines, but I try to use them for inspiration rather than subscribing to anyone else's idea of style. And when I'm feeling stale, I'll visit a gallery or go for a walk, or even see a film, immersing myself in new ideas. It's not long before inspiration finds me. Surrounding yourself with things that inspire and get the creative juices flowing is so important. Their power to make you feel happier should not be underestimated.

I want our house to be unique and exquisite to us. That other people seem to enjoy being in it as much as we do is a happy bonus and I finally feel we've created a space I could live in contentedly for the rest of my life. A home for our family, friends, pets and cherished objects. But the very concept of home is an evolving thing and I know I won't stop being creative around the house anytime soon – I'm sure we'll keep updating here and there each season, with different fabrics and whimsical items that take our fancy, as horizons inevitably broaden.

I want to make it clear that I'm not what you would call 'arty' – I'm too pragmatic. I've never seen much point in form without function, though I do think a handsome object can list its sole function as adding beauty to the world. I'm not even particularly adept with a needle or paintbrush, but I love being crafty and making simple things, borne out of long, lazy summer afternoons or winter evenings in front of the fire. And I get even more satisfaction from giving them away than keeping them, and watching friends' faces light up. It's easy to carve out time like this, and incredibly fulfilling.

Crafts need not be tacky. Think more along the lines of the gorgeous things you see in small homewares boutiques (essentially made by cottage industries) rather than something your beloved Nan would make, or naff '70s macramé plant holders and pottery ashtrays. If nothing else, this book will show you that crafts have become hip again, and share some simple ideas and skills on how to make them – even for the most complete novices. They are great fun to spend time on, particularly for or with children. And think how much pleasure you'll get from saying to admirers, 'I made it myself'.

This book follows the course of a year, sharing lots of ideas and techniques for the best things to create at different times during each season. It's also laid out this way because each time of the year is special, and making certain things at different times celebrates the change of seasons. Each project includes step-by-step instructions, and an introduction to get you in the mood for the season ahead.

*The Crafty Minx* also conveys an ethos: that things made by hand are special and hold a little bit of you in them. You *can* trust your imagination to create a beautiful environment for yourself and others. Spending even a small amount of time doing this actually restores the spirit and is much more rewarding than sitting down in front of a television after a hard day's work.

I hope *The Crafty Minx* will convince you that there's real joy to be had in making your own things, and reassure you that you already have the skills needed to get crafty. Enjoy recreating the projects and coming up with your own variations and feel free to unleash your creativity – that is where happiness lies.

*Good luck, and happy crafting!*

KELLY DOUST

# Why get creative?

When was the last time you gave or received a handmade gift? Or sat down to make something for yourself? Like the proverbial baby with the bathwater, crafts largely seem like a habit we've thrown out over the years. It's hardly surprising: the majority of us lead hectic modern lives and often feel too pressed for time to sit down and allow ourselves the necessary space to be creative. Given our distance from a time where crafts were integral to our lives, they have now developed a reputation for being 'old world' and out of fashion. We live so much in 'the now'. Perhaps this is because, unlike generations before us, we're never very far away from technology that superficially connects us to everyone else.

No wonder then, that the world of the imagination does not feel as important as the more immediate demands of work, family, friends or our relationship. But personal fulfilment is at the heart of this quadrant for a happy and balanced life, and creativity an essential element needed to achieve it. Unfortunately, most of us don't realise how very easy it is to be creative.

We are more affluent than any generation that has walked the Earth before us, with widespread access to inexpensive goods made to huge economies of scale in third-world countries. We can buy whatever we want in a store, so who needs to recycle the way our grandmothers did anymore? The answer is that we all do – yesterday.

So few products now are designed to be treasured for anything other than their monetary value, let alone given a new lease of life through recycling. And all because of our incessant desire to acquire, to consume. But appreciating our possessions, finding new uses for preloved or unwanted things and creating heirlooms for the next generation not only instils the objects surrounding us with a very human element – because handmade or cherished belongings do hold something of the essence of their maker – it also leaves a legacy for our children. It's hard

to believe that one day the resources will dry up, landfills overflowing with our waste, but it's time to get creative, before it's too late.

With many young people today growing up in households where both parents work and don't have time to teach them domestic arts such as cooking, sewing and gardening – let alone some of the more frivolous crafts – most of us barely know how to sew on a button anymore. The feminist revolution necessarily fought to give women more equality in the home and the workplace, but also rejected the idea of domesticity and since then, we've said goodbye to these skills.

A friend's mother, a very stylish woman in her mid-60s, told me recently that when she was younger, all her clothes were handmade. She remembers keenly the thrill of shopping for her first store-bought dress. 'It was such a novelty,' she said. We've come so far beyond this in a relatively short period of time. Through sheer abundance, a lot of the delight has disappeared out of our shopping trips, and although our homes are groaning under the weight of all our things, we're still not satisfied. A heightened awareness of the unsustainability of this (both emotionally and environmentally), paired with new economic pressures, underpins the modern crafts comeback.

There is a huge psychological and cultural shift taking place at the moment, towards reclaiming some of our lost domestic and creative skills, a *zeitgeist* which is steadily becoming mainstream. Think of trends towards home cooking, compacting and self-sufficiency, and the push to tear children away from overstimulating technology and back to basics; to imaginative rather than technology-aided play. It makes so much sense. We are lucky to have so many options available to us, and in a very fortunate position: we can benefit from modern technology but also enjoy the spoils of wealth, so we can spend more time with the people we care about, and more time connecting with our inner selves.

This has to be the way forward.

# Getting started

## Where to begin?

## Useful (but not essential) equipment

When embarking on any new venture in life – whether it's getting married, going on holiday, starting a business or having a baby – it's easy to get overwhelmed by all the choices you'll have to make about what you'll actually need. There's an astounding range of goods and services out there catering to almost every niche market, but the question should always be: what do I *really* need, and how much am I prepared to spend on the things I want?

The weekend papers and glossy magazines will trip over themselves to give you advice, along with long lists of 'must-haves', usually supplied by advertisers. I'm allergic to 'must-have'. My advice is: start small when it comes to making your own things. This may not be a new direction for you, but simply a nice diversion or something to dabble in – and that's okay.

Years ago, I decided I wanted to learn scuba diving. I promptly signed up for an expensive course of diving lessons, booked a trip and bought a few snazzy pieces of equipment. After scaring myself senseless during an encounter with a large fish (not even a shark, I'm afraid, just a rather large John Dory that caught me unawares) on my first ocean dive, I wasn't so keen on scuba diving and haven't really done much of it since.

Lesson learnt: work out whether you actually enjoy sewing before buying a $1400 sewing machine with matching overlocker. I'm still using the second-hand one I bought from a flea market for $35.

Buy some needles and thread to begin with, if you don't already have them, and play about with scraps of fabric from clothes you were planning to get rid of. In this book, you'll find lots of ideas for using even these most basic of items. I've refined my sewing and crafts kit after years of collecting bits and pieces and working out what I do actually

use, so I certainly wouldn't suggest you go out tomorrow and buy all the following, but these are some of the items I find most useful:

◉ Sewing machine
◉ Dressmaker's scissors (these are important: as with a cook's knife, buy the best you can afford)
◉ Tape measure
◉ Rotary cutter, quilting ruler and cutting board, for speedy patchworking
◉ Tracing paper (baking paper, at a pinch)
◉ Bobble-headed pins
◉ Sewing needles
◉ A thimble (if you are a little clumsy like me and tend to prick yourself – I usually don't bother)
◉ Larger embroidery / tapestry needles
◉ Small, sharp scissors for loose threads (also called embroidery scissors)
◉ Pinking shears (scissors with a zigzag edge: not necessary, but good for cutting fabrics that fray easily, such as canvas, linen or wool)
◉ Double-sided appliqué webbing (Vliesofix) or appliqué glue, for keeping decorative patches in place
◉ Dressmaker's chalk
◉ Quick unpick / seam ripper
◉ Standard machine needles
◉ Denim machine needles
◉ Machine needles for delicate fabrics, such as silk or organza
◉ Bobbins and bobbin case
◉ Separate bobbin winder (you don't *need* this because you can wind bobbins on your machine, but they come in handy when you're using your machine a lot)

# Basic art supplies

It's always good to have a box full of basic art supplies stored away for rainy afternoon projects, such as making collages, greeting cards or paintings. These will come in handy:

◉ Sketchbook – for drawing, jotting down ideas and creating a scrapbook of inspiring images
◉ A few artist's canvases in different shapes and sizes
◉ Staple gun and staples – for making your own canvases or showing off fabrics on their own as wall panels. These are inexpensive and useful for simple upholstery projects as well
◉ Cardboard
◉ Pencils
◉ Acrylic paints – primary colours of blue, yellow, red as well as white and black mean you can mix any other colour you need
◉ Watercolours
◉ Paintbrushes in a variety of sizes
◉ Paper glue
◉ Paper scissors

# Luxury extras

Here are some materials to move you – this is an area where you can be as thrify or as extravagant as you like, but think about collecting them as a long-term project rather than in one single mission.

- A selection of threads – black, white, beige and navy are your essentials, but it's good to build up a whole rainbow of colours for use on all fabrics. The general rule is to match thread to your fabric (cotton for cotton, silk for silk and polyester/cotton polyester for synthetics) but cotton polyester threads are sturdy and work well on most fabrics. Colour-wise, anything goes: use a contrasting colour if you want to highlight hems, or a shade darker than your fabric if you want it to blend in. A good tip is to wind half of your bobbins with basic colours at the same time, so they're ready when you need them.
- Embroidery thread, also in a range of colours – red, white, black and royal blue are a good start for lovely contrasts
- Balls of wool in colours you adore
- Cross-stitch fabric (this can be an even-weave fabric, such as linen, or special cross-stitch fabric called Aida)
- Fabrics of every colour, pattern, texture and weave under the sun
- Wool felt
- Calico
- Ribbons
- Buttons
- Rickrack
- Bias binding
- Interfacing (pure cotton, woven interfacing is preferable as the synthetic kind does not wash well)
- Polyester fibrefill or wool stuffing

# Fabulous fabrics

I have always been a natural fabric fetishist. I can't resist checking the labels on everything, to see exactly what things are made of. This might sound obsessive, but it's the only way to develop your own sensory perception and taste. After a while, it becomes second nature and you'll be able to spot a nasty acrylic jumper or polyester shirt from a few steps away without actually touching it.

Shopping for beautiful fabrics and materials is one of my favourite pastimes, but it can become very expensive, especially if you don't have a project in mind or know the exact measurements you will need. Even so, you should always be on the hunt for good fabric whenever and wherever you can, because, so often, a particular pattern or texture will provide just the inspiration you need to get started.

Don't turn your nose up at second-hand fabrics or remnants. Many of the most stylish printmakers and upholstery fabric suppliers sell remnants, ranging from tiny scraps to a few metres. A good way to get the most out of their distinctive patterns and high-quality fabrics is to mix them with less expensive materials, such as denim, canvas or calico, for the same upmarket look. Creative patchworking with small pieces also looks great and even the smallest remnants can be used with cardboard to make birthday cards or bookmarks.

Try to recognise the fabrics used all around you, and don't be afraid to rub your fingers against them to get a feel for their unique texture and suitability for different items – cashmere cardigans, cool linen shirts in summer, pashmina scarves, knobbly wool and cotton-mix sofa cushions, sturdy upholstery canvas, damask tablecloths, high thread-count Egyptian cotton sheets, lambswool and angora jumpers, the stretchy cotton jersey used in t-shirts, denim, satin, organza and the finest wisps of silk that seem like they will disintegrate at the touch.

## Why natural fabrics?

They breathe, wear well, and will see you through many washes and fashion cycles if you're lucky (cashmere will last a lifetime and longer if hand washed and properly cared for). They are more sensuous to the touch, and a good indicator of quality. Enough said.

## When are synthetic fabrics appropriate?

High-quality rayons and viscose in certain evening gowns and dress shirts, to keep them wrinkle-free; rough-and-tumble wear for children or for anything that needs to be wiped down. Your pet's favourite rug or sofa, '70s parties ... and that's about it.

*Bits & Pieces*

## Buttons, sequins, ribbons and all manner of other fripperies

I adore buttons. I love sequins, beads, ribbons, faux gems and those sparkly discs, as worn by the legendary Russian model Veruschka in 1966, too. In true bowerbird style, I see them winking at me from miles away (well, the far side of a flea market or haberdashery shop) and home in. But be warned: develop a passion for these fripperies and you will find yourself absorbed in them for hours.

My love affair with all buttons great and small began years ago. Throughout my childhood we always had half a dozen cake tins kicking about the house, filled with all manner of shiny things. I remember purloining them for the afternoon to tip out on my bedroom floor and sort by colour, shape and uniqueness, only to throw them all back together again at the end, minus a few very special ones selected as treasures. Somehow, keeping buttons sorted in their groups is never as fun as finding a perfect specimen or two in an old jam jar filled with the boring white ones clipped from shirts headed for the rag cupboard. Half the pleasure is in selecting them.

Particular favourites are the monochrome saucers once used to boldly define '60s trench coats, delicate mother-of-pearl, cashmere cardigan numbers, and most cloth-covered styles. There is something painstaking and precious about the latter – it seems few people have the time or inclination to cover the stainless steel frames anymore, to match buttons to the fabric of a home-made dress. I like the time and effort they represent, and meticulous detailing such as this is usually an indication of high quality.

# Clever things to do with buttons

- ◉ Adorn or update old sweaters, cloth clutches or anything, really
- ◉ Button paintings
- ◉ Button belts
- ◉ Jewellery – necklaces, bracelets and brooches

# Before you start sewing ...

Here are just a few terms and things that you should know:

- Casing — A wide double hem that is used to thread ribbon or elastic through.

- Clip across the corner — When you sew around a 90-degree corner, such as on a cushion cover, before turning the piece right side out, trim diagonally across each corner, close to the stitching. This reduces the bulk of fabric in the corner so that when you turn the piece right side out, your corners form neat points.

- Clip the curves — When you sew a seam around a curve, before you turn the item right side out, carefully make small snips across the seam allowance towards your stitching. Take great care not to actually snip into the stitching itself. Make these snips at 1–2 cm ($^1/_2$–$^3/_4$ in) intervals. When you turn the item right side out, the curved seam will sit nice and flat, without puckers.

- Double hem — Turn the raw edge of your fabric to the wrong side – an iron is handy for doing this – then turn under the folded edge again and stitch along the inner edge. This creates a neat hem that completely encloses the raw edge.

- Double-sided appliqué webbing — A wonderful adhesive-backed paper that enables you to cut and adhere appliqué shapes to fabric. It also seals the raw edges of the shapes, making fraying less of a problem. The only thing you need to remember is that the finished shapes will be mirror-images of the way they were traced — so if you're using letters, you need to trace them back-to-front.

- French seam — This seam is stitched in two stages. First, lay your pieces of fabric together with the *wrong* sides facing each other. Stitch a narrow seam around the edges. Now turn the piece inside out, so the *right* sides are now facing each other. Use your iron to press the seamed edges nice and flat. Stitch around the edges again, allowing a slightly wider seam allowance than before. Turn the item right side out and press again. A French seam totally encloses the raw edges of your fabric so that no fraying can occur. It is ideal for delicate fabrics, those that fray badly or for items that need frequent washing.

- **Interfacing** — A woven or non-woven fabric that is used to reinforce fabric, giving it more strength or body. It comes in a variety of thicknesses and is also available in a fusible version, which is ironed in place on the wrong side of your fabric.

- **Machine-baste** — Change the stitch length on your machine to the longest stitch available and stitch pieces together to hold them until you do the final stitching. It's the same as tacking by hand.

- **Reverse at each end** — When you sew a seam on the machine, you need to secure the threads so that the seam does not unravel. You can do this by reversing back and forth at each end of the seam. You can also pull the bobbin thread through to the front and tie off both threads by hand.

- **Right sides together** — Place your pieces together so that the outside or patterned sides are facing inwards towards each other, and the wrong sides are facing out.

- **Seam allowance** — The measurement that you need to add to the edges of your fabric when cutting to allow for stitching the seams. It can vary from 5 mm to 2 cm ($\frac{1}{4}$ in to $\frac{3}{4}$ in), depending on the fabric itself and the nature of your project. You do not need to add seam allowance to edges that will be finished with bias binding.

- **Topstitch** — A line of stitching done on the right side of the fabric. It can be used both decoratively and to add strength to seams and edges.

- **Zipper foot** — A special narrow foot for your sewing machine that allows you to sew close to the edge of the zipper teeth.

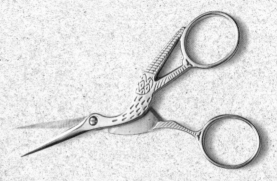

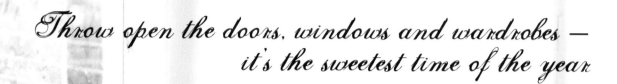

*Throw open the doors, windows and wardrobes —
it's the sweetest time of the year*

# spring

Spring is just beautiful in Australia and Sydney's customary scent of flowering jasmine, paired with cooling bitumen after a late afternoon shower, smells like home to me. In Europe, where the change of seasons is far more marked, the first decent days after months of grey have people piling onto outdoor tables at cafés and smiling for no apparent reason at strangers on the street. It was only when I lived there that I came to really understand that fine weather is a cause for celebration.

Once you appreciate how lucky we are to live in such a temperate climate, it seems criminal to be parked indoors in front of the television when it's perfect outside. But it doesn't mean you can't enjoy staying home in the warmer months. Now is the best time to get out in the garden, reinvent your wardrobe, make *pasta primavera,* decorate the house for the new season, have a garage sale or host lots of afternoon teas with friends.

Maternity hospitals are packed to the rafters nine months on from summer holidays and silly season celebrations, so host a baby shower or make beautiful gifts for new mamas and their children. Even better, whip up two extra serves of whatever you're cooking for a few nights and drop it around to any new parents in your circle. This has to be the kindest, most thoughtful gift you can offer two people who are basically too tired to cook. And trust me, they will never forget it.

One of the first things I noticed about our house when we inspected it before auction was that it was flooded with natural light for a good portion of the day. I have friends who prefer their darker, cool interiors as a retreat from the outside world, but I need to see the sky changing and have some idea of what to wear when I leave the house.

I hate the feeling of being cooped up, so I adore our tall sash windows that open wide and security doors at front and back to get a good through-breeze going. Living in a fairly quiet area, it's also reassuring to hear the sounds of the neighbourhood drifting in unobtrusively: birds, children and conversations in Greek over the back fence. I feel we have some essential privacy, but also a connection to the life of the street.

When you open up your home after any period of hibernation, whether following winter, illness or a holiday, it's a good idea to make some changes to reflect a brighter mood. This chapter is all about being inspired to look at fairly ordinary things in new ways. Spring is a time of new beginnings, so open up your home to new life, love and inspiration.

# Loud and louche doorstops

In the spirit of the season, these funky doorstops (inspired by Julie Paterson of Cloth Fabric) will help keep the good energy flowing through your home and stand out in any room with a door. They make a great gift for just about anybody and can be customised to match the surroundings, but bright colours and striking prints are best. Mix modern and vintage fabrics for a timeless look or consider patchworking smaller pieces together, backed with interfacing for strength. Interfacing also works well to strengthen softer fabrics like linen or cotton.

These doorstops have a very relaxed look and improve with age.

*Louche = elegantly wasted*

## You will need

- Two 14.5 cm (5³/₄ in) squares of canvas or sturdy upholstery fabric (or thinner fabric strengthened with interfacing)
- Four 18 x 14.5 cm (7 x 5³/₄ in) rectangles of a similar material (go matchy-matchy if you like, but I prefer five contrasting sides on my doorstops and simple denim for the underside)
- 20 cm (8 in) length for strap (35 mm-wide (1¹/₂ in)) cotton webbing or canvas ribbon)
- 2 kg (4¹/₂ lb) dry rice
- Polyester fibrefill
- Bobble-headed pins
- Sewing machine and thread
- Chopstick or ruler
- Sheet of paper
- Dressmaker's scissors
- Needle and thread

## Instructions

1. Play with your pieces of fabric until you decide which pieces look best next to each other. Your final shape is going to be like a fat brick with square ends.

2. With right sides together, pin a square between two rectangles along the 14.5 cm (5³/₄ in) edges, then pin the remaining square to the other 14.5 cm (5³/₄ in) edge of the two rectangles. This will give you a hollow rectangle.

3. Allowing 1 cm (³/₈ in) seams, stitch the pieces together as pinned.

4. Lay your top rectangle on the table, right side facing up, and place the strap across the centre from end to end, matching raw edges of strap and rectangle.

5. Sew the strap into place along the short ends, reversing back and forth for strength – the strap will need to support the doorstop's weight of 2 kg (4¹/₂ lb).

6. With right sides together, pin the top (with its strap) and bottom rectangles in place.

7. Allowing 1 cm (³/₈ in) seams, sew the top in place. This step can be a little fiddly – start sewing in the middle of one side and sew into the corner, then, with the needle in the fabric, lift the presser foot and swivel the fabric on the needle to turn the corner. Lower the presser foot again and sew to the next corner. Do the same thing at each corner until you are back to the beginning.

8. Sew the bottom rectangle in place in the same way as the top, but leave a 10 cm (4 in) opening in one long straight edge so that you can turn the cover inside out.

9. Turn your brick shape right side out through the opening. Use a chopstick or ruler to poke out the corners if you can't manage this with your fingers.

10. Curl a sheet of paper into a cone shape to make a funnel. Stick the narrow end into the opening, then pour all the rice through the funnel into the rectangular 'brick'.

11. When all the rice has been poured in, fill the rest of the shape with fibrefill, using the chopstick to fill out the edges.

12. Turn in the raw edges of the opening and pinch them together, then use your needle and thread to sew the opening closed with small firm stitches.

# Pretty peg bag

## You will need

- Tea towel
- Bias binding
- Wire coat hanger (the kind drycleaners use)
- Small amount double-sided appliqué webbing (from craft and haberdashery stores)
- Contrasting fabric for appliqué (plain for the letters and a scrap of print for a decorative motif)
- Iron
- Scrap paper and pencil
- Sharp paper scissors and dressmaker's scissors
- Needle and sewing thread
- Bobble-headed pins
- Dressmaker's chalk
- Sewing machine and thread
- Pinking shears

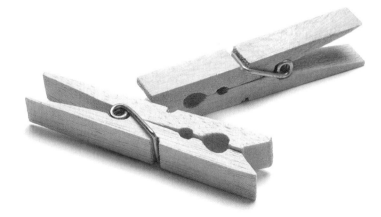

Peg bags are the perfect example of taking a boring, utilitarian item and injecting some style into it. Washing lines look gorgeous decorated with paper-cut doilies or chains of paper dolls when you're entertaining in the garden, but this peg bag will also turn your line into a 'feature'. Who'd have thunk it?

This '50s-inspired peg bag has been made out of an old tea towel. I covered a burn mark with the appliqué roses and some pink paint from another messy project with the appliquéd letters.

## *Instructions*

1. Stitch a row of bias binding to both the top and bottom edges of the tea towel to bind the edges.

2. Lay the tea towel flat on the table with the wrong side facing up. Fold down the top edge by about 14 cm (5½ in) – this measurement should be the height of your coat hanger from its bottom to the base of the neck. Fold up the lower edge of the tea towel to meet the bias binding on the top edge. The bound edges will form the opening of the finished bag. Use your iron to press these folds to mark their position.

3. Sketch large simple letters P, E, G, S onto scrap paper.

4. Appliqué webbing has a smooth paper side and a slightly rough glue side. Trace each of the letters – back-to-front – onto the paper side of your appliqué webbing. With paper scissors, cut out each letter separately, leaving a 6 mm (¼ in) margin of paper around your traced line.

5. Using your iron, press each letter, glue-side down this time, onto the wrong side of your plain appliqué fabric. At the same time, press a piece of webbing onto the wrong side of the decorative motif. The webbing should be large enough to cover the area of the motif with a small margin around the edges.

6. Using fabric scissors, cut out the letters accurately around the traced lines, and cut out the motif around the edges of the design.

7. Carefully peel away and discard the backing paper on the letters and position them in the correct order on the right side of the folded tea towel (they will now be the right way round), so they are centred just below the bias binding opening.

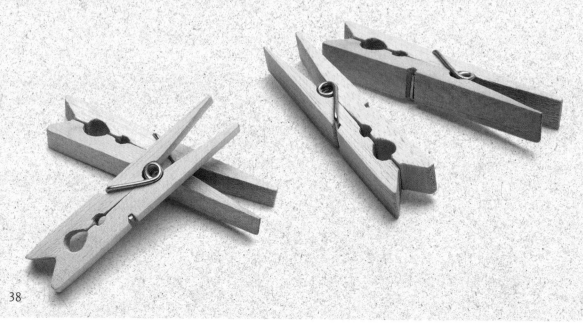

*Tip*

Tie a small ribbon bow around the hook for a pretty finishing touch.

8. Position the decorative motif on the top half of the folded tea towel so that it is centred just above the opening.

9. Use your iron to press the letters and motif in place – the heat of the iron melts the glue and the appliqué fabrics will adhere firmly to the background.

10. Although the webbing will keep the appliqué firmly in place, for extra strength and decoration, work small straight stitches around the edges of the letters and motif, using a needle and thread.

11. Now, re-fold the tea towel along the pressed fold lines so that the wrong sides are facing out, with the appliqué on the inside. Pin the side edges together to hold them.

12. Lay your coat hanger on the top section so that the hook is centred. Make a mark in the top edge where you need to cut a tiny hole for the hook and trace the outline of the hanger's sloping sides onto the fabric with your chalk.

13. Set the coat hanger aside. Starting at the lower fold, stitch the side edges together on the lower bag section, then stitch across the edges of the opening and stitch along the traced outline to the top fold.

14. Repeat for the other side.

15. Use your pinking shears to trim away the excess fabric on the shaped top section and snip a tiny hole for the hook in the centre top where you marked it.

16. Turn the bag right side out and manoeuvre the hanger back into the bag, carefully working the hook through the hole at the top.

17. If you want to, you can make a line of stitching through both layers of fabric just under the sloping arms of the hanger to secure it in place – but if you think your bag is going to need a wash now and then, it's easier to leave it unstitched.

18. Post your pegs into the letterbox slot at the front and hang on the clothesline.

While winter is the time for burning oils and musky-scented candles in your home, nothing beats the scent of fresh flowers in spring. It's not always easy to find the time to get to your favourite florist or flower market for supplies, so one solution is to chop a few stems from flowers in the garden and put them in small vases around the home. My front garden is filled with star jasmine and gardenia; both flower in spring and smell like heaven.

Chop a few stems from the garden and place them in candle holders or small bottles in each room, changing every few days once they wilt. I use recycled red bitters bottles from my local Italian deli. Another option is to plant window boxes; that way, you only need to open up a window for beautiful scents to float in on the breeze.

Don't be put off from planting whatever you like the look and smell of in window boxes or even mixing different plants together in the one pot (providing they fit). Forget the geraniums and be a bit more adventurous. I figure that even if you have to replace plants every few months, they will still last longer than cut flowers and can usually be transplanted to the garden once they've stopped flowering.

# Wild window boxes

## Tips for window boxes

- ✿ Bulbs are great for one cycle of flowers, but plants that will flower again next year can be transplanted to the garden for their greenery in the interim.
- ✿ Base your choices on scent (jasmine, roses, gardenia) or appearance (anemones, fuchsia, chrysanthemums).
- ✿ Use a watering can on well-drained window boxes every couple of days, or at the end of every day during hot, dry spells. Try to use 'grey water' (water collected from the shower, bath or sink after you've done a load of dishes).
- ✿ Use a good seaweed-based fertiliser every few weeks, and a slow-release hydrating fertiliser (especially important in hotter climates).

# 'Spring is Here' shopper bag

## Tip
You could add a pretty, personalised feature, such as an interesting vintage button or ribbons to close the bag's opening.

## You will need

- Approximately 0.7 m x 112 cm-wide ($3/4$ yd x 44 in) sturdy fabric, such as upholstery fabric in cotton or a cotton/linen mix
- Measuring tape or ruler
- Fabric scissors
- Sewing machine and thread
- Iron
- Bobble-headed pins

This is for all the extra market shopping you'll be doing now the days are getting longer. Shopper bags are more environmentally friendly than the plastic kind, which are likely to be phased out over the next few years anyway. Make one for yourself or as a gift for a friend; far more stylish than the green cloth ones commonly sold in supermarkets, they also fold up nicely in the bottom of your handbag. Size is completely up to you, but a finished bag of 35 x 35 cm (14 x 14 in) is most useful: not so small you can't fit a carton of milk, a loaf of bread and some fruit and vegies in it, but not so big you'll dislocate your shoulder carrying it when full.

## *Instructions*

1. Measure and cut two 40 cm (16 in) squares of fabric.

2. From the leftover fabric, measure and cut two straps, each 12 x 78 cm (4³/₄ x 31 in). This is a good size for full straps that don't cut into your shoulder and allow enough space to carry comfortably under your arm.

3. With *wrong* sides together and allowing 6 mm (¹/₄ in) seams, sew the squares together around three edges. Trim diagonally across the seam allowance on the lower corners and turn the bag inside out, so the right sides are now together.

4. With *right* sides together, stitch around the sides and bottom edge again, this time allowing a 1 cm (³/₈ in) seam allowance. (This double seam is called a French seam and gives a very strong, non-fray finish.)

5. To create boxed corners, fold the lower corner into a point so that the side seam is centred at the apex and aligned with the bottom seam. Measure 4 cm (1¹/₂ in) down the seam from the apex and rule a straight line across the corner at this point. Sew across the ruled line, securing the stitching firmly at each end. Make another line of stitching close to the first for strength. Do not trim off the corner.

6. Repeat Step 5 for the opposite corner.

7. Using your iron, press under 1 cm (³/₈ in) around the remaining raw edge at the top of the bag, then press under another 1 cm (³/₈ in) and stitch this hem in place close to the inner fold, creating a neat opening edge. Leave the bag inside out at this stage.

8. Fold each strap in half lengthwise, right sides together, and stitch along the length, allowing a 1 cm (³/₈ in) seam. Leave both short ends open.

9. With your iron, press the tube so that the seam you have just stitched runs down the centre of the strap (rather than on the edge) and press the seam allowance open.

10. Stitch across one short end. Trim diagonally across the seam allowance on the corners and turn the straps right side out.

11. Turn under the raw edges on the open end of each strap and press. Topstitch around the edges of the straps, stitching 3 mm (¹/₈ in) from the edge.

12. On each side of the bag, measure 7 cm (2³/₄ in) in from each side seam and mark with a pin for your strap positions. With the right side of the strap facing the wrong side of the bag, pin the ends of the straps in place on the inside of the bag. Check that you've got all your right and wrong sides facing correctly, then stitch the straps firmly in place, working a small square or rectangle of stitching, with intersecting diagonal lines, for extra strength.

13. Turn the bag inside out – you now have a fully finished shopper bag.

# Vintage silk scarf cushions

Second-hand silk scarves are cheap and easy to find in flea markets because so few people wear them anymore. Luxury designer labels such as Hermés still design and sell new ones, but I'm sure that apart from with the elite jet set, they are headed the way of the dodo. I have a whole box of delicate silk scarves from other eras in every colour imaginable, which I have to remind myself to raid every few months to add flair to an outfit. They're easy to forget about, but silk scarves really do add to any look, and there is something supremely polished about one knotted about the neck, waist or even wrapped around the wrist like a cuff.

I have been on the hunt for a particular vintage silk scarf for months now, with a map on it, like the kind you see in atlases showing all the regions and cities and towns of each country. When I find it I'm going to turn it into a cushion, and evoke a look somewhere between a men-only cigar bar and the private den of a millionaire's yacht in my living room (even for just a moment, and even if the only person who understands this inspiration is me).

## You will need

- Silk scarf
- 53 cm (21 in) square lightweight non-fusible interfacing
- 53 x 56 cm (21 x 22 in) denim or upholstery fabric
- 45 cm (18 in) zipper
- 50 cm (20 in) cushion insert
- Iron
- Needle and thread
- Ruler
- Dressmaker's chalk
- Sewing machine and thread
- Sewing machine zipper foot
- Fabric scissors or pinking shears

# Instructions

1. Using your iron, press the silk scarf carefully.

2. Centre the interfacing square on the wrong side of the scarf and pin in place. Use your needle and thread to tack the interfacing to the scarf to hold it in position.

3. Trim the edges of the scarf to match the interfacing.

4. Measure and cut your denim rectangle into two pieces: one should be 53 x 14.5 cm (21 x 5³/₄ in) and the other should be 53 x 41.5 cm (21 x 16¹/₄ in).

5. With right sides together, align the two backing pieces along the 53 cm (21 in) edge.

6. Take your zip and lay it along this 53 cm (21 in) edge so that it is equidistant from both ends. Make a mark on the edges of the fabric to show where the zip opening should start and finish.

7. Put the zip aside and, allowing a 1.5 cm (⁵/₈ in) seam, sew the seam closed at each end, from your mark to the edge, leaving the seam open in the middle. Press the seam allowance open, pressing open the edges of the unstitched section as well.

8. With the right side of the fabric facing upwards, position your closed zip under the opening (make sure it's facing up the right way) and pin it in place. Pin one folded edge of the opening about 2 mm (¹/₁₆ in) from the zipper teeth and the pin the other side about 1 cm (³/₈ in) from the folded edge. Place a pin across the seam at the top and bottom of the opening, one pin just above the pull tab and the other just below the zip stop. It is a good idea to tack the zip in position before stitching it, as the pins can get a bit awkward while you stitch.

9. Using a zipper foot on your machine, sew the zip in place, stitching along both sides and pivoting on the needle at the corners to stitch across the top and bottom too.

10. Open the zip slightly. With right sides together, raw edges matching and allowing a 1.5 cm (⁵/₈ in) seam, stitch the silk cushion front to the back around all edges.

11. To reduce bulk, carefully cut away the seam allowance of the interfacing to about 2 mm (¹/₁₆ in). Remove basting if it shows. Clip diagonally across each corner to remove the extra fabric – take care not to cut into your stitching – and turn the cover right side out through the zip opening. Push the corners out with your fingers.

12. Insert the cushion pad into your cover and zip it up. Make several of these with dreamy, pastel scarves and scatter around your boudoir for a breezy vibe.

# Tip

* If the thought of inserting a zip is putting you off making your own cushion covers, you can make a lapped back opening (see the Patchwork Cushions on page 177). Alternatively, just leave out the zip and cut the back the same size as the front. Leave one side open for the cushion pad and sew the opening edges of the cover together by hand when you've finished. It surely won't need washing all that often, and when it does, simply unpick the seam and sew it up again.

# *Framed collages*

## *You will need*

- ◎ A frame, salvaged from a market or charity shop (it doesn't need glass or the backing board)
- ◎ Paint and brush (if required)
- ◎ 5 mm-thick ($^1/_4$ in) corkboard to fit frame (from a craft shop or hardware store)
- ◎ Stanley knife
- ◎ Staple gun
- ◎ Thick cardboard backing (cut from large cartons)
- ◎ Small nails or masking tape
- ◎ A collection of your favourite cards, photos, ticket stubs or anything you want to pin to the board
- ◎ Drawing pins

A collage does not necessarily need to be fixed to paper or canvas — the idea behind this project is to turn a pin board into an art form. Collect your favourite items and array them however you like within a second-hand frame. A collection of photographs, cards, letters, ribbons, ticket stubs (or any other items you like) will bring to mind good memories and can be quite inspiring, which is why this works well when hung above a work desk in a home office or study. And the best thing is that you can keep switching the pieces around within the frame to suit your mood or evoke a current inspiration.

## Instructions

1. If your frame is looking a bit ratty, give it a lick of paint. You might also want to paint the frame to better suit the room you'll be hanging it in.

2. Using your Stanley knife, cut the corkboard to the exact size of the rebate of the frame.

3. Insert the cork into the frame from the back, and use your staple gun to secure it in place. 3–5 staples for each side should be enough.

4. Now cut one or two thicknesses of cardboard to fit behind the cork to make a thicker depth for pinning into. Secure in place with a small nail in each corner or with masking tape around the edges.

5. Take all the pieces you've collected for your collage, and arrange them over your cork board. Start pinning them in place for the most visually arresting layout.

6. Hang the finished work above your work desk, in your kitchen, above your dressing table or anywhere else you need some daily inspiration.

*For the newcomers*

# Welcoming little people into the world

It's not until you actually have a child (or at least, I wasn't privy to this until after I'd had my own), that you realise how generous people are when it comes to babies. When my husband and I had our daughter, Olive, we felt like we'd barely sent out the message of her birth before flowers and gifts of all sorts started arriving at the hospital. It was quite overwhelming.

The day we left to go home was also very emotional. We kept expecting security to tackle us to the ground as we walked out the door. I've heard this is a common feeling for new parents. After four days of kid-glove care from the midwives, my obstetrician and the paediatrician, our emotions got the better of us and we couldn't stop crying. I know it's a cliché, but our house finally felt like a home once she had arrived in it.

In those early weeks, friends also started turning up unannounced, not to stay and meet our new babe, but to unobtrusively drop off elaborate meals and boxes of food and goodies – magazines, herbal teas and delicious fresh fruit or chocolates – making us feel utterly spoiled. Packages of clothes and toys seemed to arrive every day and I didn't know when I was going to get the time to thank everyone appropriately. It made me realise how rubbish we'd been in the past when our friends had their own babies.

In our society, where people are so busy most days, I think it's extra important that we take the time to honour the birth of a child and stop to think about how special it is for the family welcoming them into the world. This almost surreal time is gone so quickly before routine sets in and the wonder of new life starts to feel 'normal'. In this instance, a little help from friends and thoughtful behaviour goes such a long way, and will be cherished for many years to come.

# A Maltese bow for a modern entrance

## You will need

- Approximately 1.5 m x 50 cm (1²/₃ yd x 20 in) fabric in pink or blue
- Sewing machine and thread
- Needle and thread

## Instructions

1. Fold your length of fabric in half lengthwise, right sides together, giving a folded piece that measures 150 x 25 cm (60 x 10 in).

2. Allowing a 1 cm (³/₈ in) seam, stitch across one short side, then pivot on the needle and stitch along the long edge until you get about half way. Leave an opening of about 10 cm (4 in), then finish stitching along the long edge, pivot on the needle and sew the second short end.

3. Turn the bow right side out through the opening, pushing out the corners into sharp points with your fingers.

4. Turn under the seam allowance on the raw edges on the opening and stitch the opening closed with a needle and thread.

5. Press the finished length well.

6. Tie your length of fabric into a neat bow, puffing up the edges of the loops and smoothing down the centre so it looks like something you'd see in a window display of a chic department store.

7. Your bow is now ready to be attached to the front door with a drawing pin or staple gun.

Every culture has its own mores when it comes to announcing the birth of a child, but I love the idea of this one, which is practised in Malta. When a baby is born on the small Mediterranean island, new parents or their families place a large pink or blue bow on the front door to announce the new arrival. It seems such a lovely way to convey the message, 'Our baby's here and we'll be ready for visitors soon.'

Make this simple cotton bow (in each colour) for any expectant parents you know. They can be kept at the ready near the front door to announce the news to the neighbourhood.

# Beautiful beanies

One of the many preoccupations of any new parent is wondering if they are keeping their newborn warm or cool enough. Babies can't regulate their own body heat, so it's up to mum and dad to swaddle or strip them of any unnecessary clothing for those first few months. And as with adults, the most heat is lost through their heads.

Use this cute cotton mini-beanie to protect a new baby's wee noggin from cold in the evening or sunburn during the day, as it's impossible to find sunhats tiny enough for a newborn. A beanie is useful on that first trip home from the hospital as, apart from their grand entrance in the delivery room, this is probably their first venture into the outside environment. At this stage, babies are very sensitive to any change in their surroundings.

Cut up an old t-shirt softened by many washes and you should have more than enough material left over to make one in a larger size when they get bigger. Give it a few months, and you'll be making one almost double the size.

## Tip

✲ How about appliquéing the little one's first initial (*M* is for Milo; *P* is for Poppy) on the front to make it extra special? If you decide to do this, it's easier to complete the appliqué on one section of the beanie before sewing all the pieces together – but remember to leave room for seam allowances.

## You will need

- ⊙ Four 13 x 17 cm (5 x 6³/₄ in) rectangles soft, stretchy cotton jersey fabric
- ⊙ Dressmaker's chalk
- ⊙ Sewing machine and thread
- ⊙ Needle and thread for hand-stitching

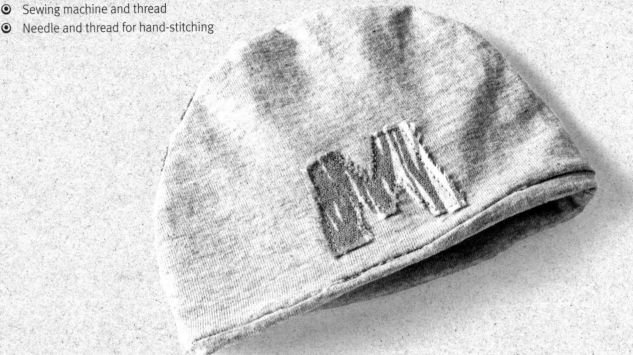

## Instructions

1. Use the edge of a saucer to trace a rounded edge onto one of the fabric rectangles, leaving one 17 cm (6³/₄ in) side straight. Cut out this beanie shape and use it as a pattern to trim the remaining three rectangles to the same rounded shape.

2. With right sides together and allowing a 6 mm (¹/₄ in) seam, sew two of your beanie shapes together around the curved edge, leaving the lower straight edge open.

3. Reverse a few times at either end for strength.

4. Sew the two remaining beanie shapes together in the same way, to create the lining.

5. With their seams aligning, put the beanie inside the beanie lining so that their right sides are facing each other and their raw edges are matching.

6. Allowing a 6 mm (¹/₄ in) seam, sew around the circumference, leaving a 3–4 cm (1–1¹/₂ in) opening in the seam.

7. Turn the beanie right side out through the opening – all the seams should now be on the inside.

8. Turn under the raw edges on the opening and neatly sew the edges together with a needle and thread.

9. Tuck one half of the beanie (the lining) into the outer layer. The beanie is designed to be worn with the seams at either ear.

# Drool-tastic bibs

## You will need

- Small piece patterned fabric for appliqué swatch
- 25 cm (10 in) square soft, stretchy cotton jersey fabric
- 25 cm (10 in) square soft towelling (cut up a face flannel if you like)
- 0.6 m x 15 mm-wide ($^2/_3$ yd x $^5/_8$ in) grosgrain ribbon
- Pinking shears
- Bobble-headed pins
- Needle and thread
- Dressmaker's scissors
- Dressmaker's chalk
- Sewing machine and thread

If you've spent any time with a baby, you'll know they're pretty messy eaters. A bib is the safest option for protecting their (and your) clothes, and to stop busy mamas doing any more loads of washing than is absolutely necessary.

Like the little beanies, these uncomplicated bibs can be made from old t-shirts. Cut around any holes or marks on the fabric, and patch an attractive swatch of fabric to the front to elevate this useful item from the solely utilitarian.

## Instructions

1. Take your small piece of patterned fabric and cut around the desired image with your pinking shears.

2. Place this at the centre of the jersey fabric square and hold it in place with a pin. Sew around the edges of the motif with your needle and thread, using small stitches close to the pinked edge.

3. Once you have completed the appliqué, pin the jersey square on top of the towelling square, right sides together.

4. Using the edge of a cup as a guide, trace and cut a small semicircle from the top of your double fabric to allow the bib to fit around the curve of the baby's neck.

5. Use a saucer or small plate to trace around the corners of the bib.

6. Cut the ribbon in half, cutting one end of each piece at an angle to prevent fraying.

7. With the raw edges matching, position the straight edge of each length of ribbon between the two pieces of fabric at either side of the neck area, then pin into place.

8. Allowing a 6 mm ($\frac{1}{4}$ in) seam, sew the two layers of fabric together around all edges, removing the pins as you sew across the ribbon ends and taking care not to catch the angled ends of the ribbon in the seam as you sew. Leave a 5 cm (2 in) opening in one side for turning.

9. Turn your fabric 'bag' right out so the appliqué is facing outwards.

10. Turn under the raw edges on the opening and neatly sew the edges together with a needle and thread.

11. Press the bib, then topstitch around the finished edge, about 3 mm ($\frac{1}{8}$ in) from the edge. The bib is now ready for the little one's next feed.

# Appliquéd singlets

## You will need

- Small piece of fabric for appliqué swatch
- One baby singlet
- Pinking shears
- Bobble-headed pins
- Needle and thread for hand-stitching

## Instructions

1. Take your small piece of fabric and cut into a square, circle or around the motif with your pinking shears.

2. Place this on the front of the singlet at the centre, and pin or tack it in place.

3. Sew around the edges with your needle and thread, working small stitches close to the pinked edge. A contrasting thread or one that picks up the colours in the appliqué will look striking and show up the homespun charm of hand stitching.

There is a reason why art galleries usually sport whitewashed walls – white is the perfect backdrop to almost any colour, and makes items displayed against it pop.

Buy a small stack of white or pastel singlets in newborn sizes (oooo to ooo) and keep them in the cupboard for new baby announcements. Collect small swatches of fabric in cute colours or patterns, with images that take your fancy – cars, roses, or anything non-gender specific, such as trees or bees – to adorn the front. Wrap simply with brown paper and a beautiful ribbon, and you have a gift that will be ready in minutes.

## Tip

You can also tie a small bow in a scrap of pretty ribbon and stitch the bow to the front of a singlet (see page 51). Make sure you stitch it very firmly, both through the knot and with a stitch or two in the loops and ends, so that it can't possibly work its way loose.

# Personalised baby linen pouch

## You will need

- 50 x 100 cm (20 x 40 in) simple cotton fabric
- Scrap of contrasting fabric, for appliqué
- 1.5 m x 20 mm-wide (1²/₃ yds x ⁷/₈ in) grosgrain ribbon
- Bobble-headed pins
- Sewing machine and thread
- Pinking shears
- Iron
- Large safety pin
- Dressmaker's chalk
- Sewing needle and thread

Baby clothes are so cute and tiny, it's easy for them to get lost in the wash (especially little socks – think about how often your own go missing and multiply that by ten ...). A linen pouch slung over the edge of the change table or cot is a great idea for keeping incy-wincy clothes separate until they're ready for the washing machine.

# Instructions

1. Fold your fabric in half crosswise, right sides together, and pin at the edges to give a 50 cm (20 in) square.

2. Allowing 1 cm ($^3/_8$ in) seams, stitch the sides of the square together, leaving 4 cm ($1^7/_8$ in) unstitched at the top of one side. Trim the seam allowance at the sides with pinking shears to prevent fraying. Press under the seam allowance on each side of the unstitched section.

3. Press under 1 cm ($^3/_8$ in) on the raw edge around the top, then press under another 3 cm ($1^1/_4$ in) and stitch this hem in place close to the inner pressed edge.

4. Turn the bag right side out. You should have a 3 cm ($1^1/_4$ in) opening in the casing at the top of one side seam.

5. Take your ribbon and large safety pin and, using the pin on the end of the ribbon, thread the ribbon through the drawstring entry with your safety pin, guiding the pin through the tube until you reach the exit again.

6. Knot the two ends of the ribbon together or – if you want to be extra neat – lap the ends over each other and secure with several stitches, then pull the join around into the casing so it can't be seen.

7. Use the chalk to draw the baby's initial on a scrap of contrasting fabric. Cut the initial out – with pinking shears if you like – and pin it to the centre of one side of the bag.

8. Stitch it in place with machine-zigzag or small hand-stitching.

9. You could also consider tracing the baby's name or initial and embroidering over the outline with a chain stitch (see page 264), if you prefer.

# Cuddle-friendly soft toys

You don't even need to be crafty with a needle and thread to make a stuffed toy for a child. Think about it: if a five-year-old can make an utterly charming sock monkey, you can too. Wouldn't it be special if your toy became a lifelong friend, and ended up living on their bed well into adulthood? I can't imagine a better gift than that.

Think about the shape you want to create; it could be an animal (cat, monkey, rabbit, elephant) or something more abstract (microbe, pillow with eyes, face with ears). It doesn't need to make sense.

My friend Carol gave us a 'Noonoo' felt blanket when Olive was born. Beautifully soft, it's shaped like a pizza but has a small pocket and odd bits and pieces of felt and embroidery sewn onto it and sprouting off in all directions. It's odd-looking but feels wonderful, and I can just see it being adopted as a security blanket. Something this unusual is quite special.

## You will need

- Scraps of woollen jumpers – keep all your leftovers from other projects
- Buttons for eyes and noses (see Tip)
- Embroidery thread and needle for creating facial expressions or personal touches, such as initials
- Pure wool stuffing
- Scrap of ribbon, for neck bow (optional)
- Scrap paper for pattern (for the cat-face pillow, on page 263)
- Dressmaker's scissors
- Needle and sewing thread, for hand-stitching

# Instructions: Monkey

1. Cut two rectangles of wool fabric, each about 8 x 15 cm ($3^1/4$ x 6 in), for your monkey's arms, two rectangles, 8 x 18 cm ($3^1/4$ x 7 in), for legs, and one rectangle, 7 x 20 cm ($2^3/4$ x 8 in), for the tail. When you're cutting into the woollen fabric, the greatest stretch should be running crossways (that is, around the limbs), rather than along the length.

2. Fold the pieces in half lengthways, right sides together and, allowing a 3 mm ($1/8$ in) seam, stitch by hand along one long side and around one of the shorter ends, sewing the short end into a curved shape as you work.

3. Turn the limbs and tail right side out and stuff with wool. Set aside.

4. Cut two 10 cm (4 in) squares of wool for the head.

5. Pin them right sides together and trim off the corners to make a rounded shape.

6. Sew around the edge, as for the limbs, leaving an opening in the bottom edge.

7. Cut a piece of wool, about 17 cm long x 21 cm wide ($6^3/4$ x $8^1/4$ in), for the body.

8. Fold the piece in half lengthways and sew the edges together to make a tube, rounding the corners at both top and bottom of the tube, to narrow the opening.

9. Fold the tube so that the seam is positioned at the centre back, then stitch along one of the shorter edges.

10. Turn the body right side out and stuff it quite firmly with wool.

11. Position the head opening over the neck opening. Using a needle and double sewing thread, sew the head firmly to the body. Before you finish stitching, stuff in a bit more wool so that the neck edge is firmly stuffed – this will prevent the head from being too floppy.

12. Stitch the open edge of the arms, legs and tail to the body, making sure your stitching is very firm and that you end off securely.

13. To make the ears, cut four rectangles, each about 5 cm (2 in) square.

14. With right sides together, stitch the ears together in pairs, rounding the edges on three sides and leaving the fourth straight edge open. Trim off excess fabric and turn ears right side out.

15. Turn in the raw edges on the straight side of the ears and stitch an ear firmly to each side of the head – remember they must be very firmly stitched so that they cannot be pulled or chewed off.

16. Cut an oval from a darker shade of wool, about 3.5 cm high x 5 cm wide ($1^1/2$ x 2 in), and sew this to the middle of the monkey's face, leaving a small opening so you can stuff in just a little more wool before stitching it closed.

17. If you are using them, stitch buttons to the monkey's face to create the eyes and nose. Alternatively, embroider features with thread.

18. Embroider a brow, smile and belly button on your monkey to give him his unique personality. Embroider a line of running stitch around the edge of each ear, through both layers, about 6 mm ($1/4$ in) from the edge.

# *Instructions: Rabbit*

1. From wool fabric, cut two rectangles, each about 8 x 10 cm ($3^{1}/_{4}$ x 4 in), for your rabbit's arms, and two rectangles, each about 10 x 15 cm (4 x 6 in), for its legs.

2. Fold the pieces in half lengthways, right sides together, and allowing a 3 mm ($^{1}/_{8}$ in) seam, stitch by hand along one long side and around one of the shorter ends, sewing the short end into a curved shape as you work.

3. Turn the limbs right side out, stuff with wool and set aside.

4. Cut two 10 cm (4 in) squares of wool for the head.

5. Pin them right sides together and trim off the corners to make a rounded shape.

6. Sew around the edge, as for the limbs, leaving an opening in the bottom edge.

7. Turn right side out, stuff with wool and set aside.

8. Cut a piece of wool, about 18 x 20 cm (7 x 8 in), to make the body.

9. Fold the piece in half lengthways and sew along the longer edge to make a tube.

10. Fold the tube so that the seam is positioned at the centre back, then stitch along one of the shorter edges.

11. Turn the body right side out and stuff it firmly with wool.

12. Position the head opening over the neck opening. Using a needle and double sewing thread, sew the head firmly to the body. Before you finish stitching, stuff in a bit more wool so that the neck edge is firmly stuffed – this will prevent the head of the toy from being too floppy.

13. Stitch the open edge of the arms and legs to the body, making sure your stitching is very firm and that you end off securely.

14. To make the ears, cut two rectangles, each about 6 cm ($2^{1}/_{2}$ in) square.

15. Fold them in half and stitch the edges, as for the limbs, rounding one short edge and leaving the remaining short edge open.

16. Turn right side out and stuff with wool.

17. Using a needle and double sewing thread, stitch the ears firmly to the top of the head – remember they must be very firmly stitched so that they can't be chewed off.

18. If you are using them, stitch buttons to the rabbit's face for eyes. Alternatively, embroider features with thread.

19. Embroider the nose, mouth and belly button on your rabbit to give him his unique personality.

20. Tie a bow round the neck, if you wish, stitching it firmly in place if the toy is for a baby.

## Instructions: Cat-face pillow

1. Using the diagram on page 263, measure and sketch a pattern piece on scrap paper.

2. Using your pattern, cut two face shapes from a jumper, remembering to add seam allowance all round to each piece when cutting. The greatest stretch should run across the cat's face.

3. With right sides together and allowing 6 mm ($^1/_4$ in) seams, sew the two pieces together around the edges, leaving a small opening at the bottom.

4. Turn right side out and stuff with wool.

5. Turn in the raw edges on the opening and stitch the opening closed.

6. Cut two small triangles of contrast wool for the inner ears.

7. Stitch the inner ears firmly in place on the cat's head.

8. Stitch on two big buttons for the eyes – or embroider the features, if you prefer.

9. Embroider a mouth, nose and whiskers. Your cat-face pillow is a perfect cuddle toy for a little one, or a soft place to rest his or her head.

# Delicious baby blankets

There's a tendency with quilts to pop them in the 'too hard' basket and assume you need special skills to complete a handsome version of your own. I confess to the same tendency but in truth, anything goes with putting together a quilt and the more unique the better.

Making a baby blanket is the easiest of all. Not only is it smaller, but you don't need to fuss with any zips or padding for this simple version, which can be used in a cot to cover a swaddled baby or laid on the carpet for them to roll around on.

Collect pretty pieces of soft fabric in wool, cotton or jersey to construct a unique and personalised blanket for a new babe. Take inspiration from a colour or a pattern for your theme (remember there's no need to stick to the tired route of pink or blue) or make 'no rules' your theme, blending together a wild range of clashing prints and colours in retro fabrics for inspired playtime.

## You will need

- About 1 m (39 in) square soft backing fabric, such as a flannelette flat sheet or wool fabric
- Square or rectangular patches of fabric, enough to make a finished size to match your flat sheet
- Rickrack
- Pinking shears
- Sewing machine and thread
- Iron

## Instructions

1. Iron your sheet or backing fabric, lay it out on the floor and trim it to your desired size. You can make a square blanket or a cot-sized one of about 80 x 90 cm ($31^{1}/_{2}$ x $35^{1}/_{2}$ in).

2. Arrange the patchwork pieces over the backing until you are happy with how they all work together. Cover the entire expanse of fabric, keeping in mind that you will need a little extra around the edges for seams. Remember too, especially if you are a beginner, that it is easier to keep to large pieces and regular shapes, such as squares and rectangles.

3. Use your pinking shears to trim the edges of all your fabric pieces – this should stop them from fraying.

4. With right sides together and allowing 6 mm ($^{1}/_{4}$ in) seams, start sewing the patchwork pieces to each other to make the top part of the blanket. You might find it easier to iron each section as you complete it, pressing the seams open or to one side, depending on what seems least bulky.

5. When you've sewn all your patchwork pieces together, turn your completed piece of fabric over and iron it flat.

6. Snip away any loose threads.

7. Line up the patchwork sheet with your flat sheet, right sides together.

8. Sew around the edges, leaving one short end open.

9. Turn the quilt right side out and gently use your fingers to push the corners out.

10. Turn in the raw edges on the opening and pin them together. Stitch the opening closed on the machine, then continue topstitching around the outer edge, pivoting on the needle at the corners.

11. If you intend for the blanket to be used more on the floor, use your rickrack to decorate around all four sides of the top of the quilt and topstitch it in place through both layers of fabric. You can also decorate one short edge of the backing fabric so that when the blanket is turned back in the cot, you will see a portion of the backing and cute rickrack edging. See!? It's nothing short of delicious.

### Tip

If you find that your blanket is 'ballooning' out, you can join the backing to the front by a method called 'tying'. Using embroidery cotton, take a stitch through both layers at various points, then knot the threads firmly on the top or back, and trim the ends into little tufts.

# Colourful crib mobile

Colour and movement fascinate small babies. You could literally suspend pieces of coloured paper from string, open a window and a baby would be transfixed for hours, but we can do better than that: here's a mobile inspired by the nonsensical nursery rhyme, *The Owl and the Pussycat*. Using recycled wire coat hangers and fabric off-cuts, play with shapes and ideas to come up with your own theme or use the following instructions to re-create this one.

## You will need

- Fabric off-cuts in red, grey, green and yellow
- Pure wool stuffing
- An assortment of buttons for eyes and noses
- Embroidery needle and thread
- Fabric scraps, for details
- Pliers
- Wire coat hanger (from the drycleaner)
- Bias binding in fuchsia or red
- Sturdy cotton thread
- Sewing machine and thread
- Dressmaker's scissors
- Chopstick
- Sewing needle and thread

## Instructions

1. Cut your fabric off-cuts into the basic shapes on pages 265–267: red for Puss, grey for Mr Owl, green for their 'beautiful pea-green boat' and yellow for the man in the moon. You will need two pieces of fabric for each.

2. With wrong sides together (you are stitching on the right side of the fabric) and allowing 6 mm (¼ in) seams, sew around the outside of the shapes. Use a contrast sewing thread to highlight the stitching. Leave a small opening at the bottom of each shape.

3. Insert wool stuffing, using the chopstick to make sure you get stuffing into every part. The boat and the moon should not be too firmly stuffed and should sit flatter than the owl and the pussycat. (Don't worry about the edges fraying – the mobile is not going to be handled once it's hanging and a little fraying on the edges just adds to the naïve charm.) Stitch the openings closed on the machine.

4. Sew the owl and the pussycat to either end of the boat, positioning the pussycat at the back and the owl at the front.

5. Sew button eyes onto the owl, pussycat and moon, reserving the largest for the owl.

6. With the embroidery needle and thread, sew on whiskers, noses and facial expressions. Stitch on small fabric details, such as a wing or bow tie, if you like.

7. With your pliers, cut the bottom straight section from the wire coat hanger.

8. Cut a piece of bias binding slightly longer than the length of wire. Fold the binding in half lengthwise and sew the long edges together to create a narrow tube.

9. Thread the wire through the tube, then trim the excess binding and neatly sew the edges closed at either end. Bend the covered wire into a gentle curve.

10. Use embroidery thread to suspend the owl and pussycat in the boat from one end of the covered wire, and the moon from the other end, suspending the moon on a shorter thread so that it is higher than the boat.

11. Attach a thin length of sturdy cotton thread to the wire to suspend the mobile, moving it along the wire until the figures balance.

12. Hang the mobile from a hook in the ceiling (well out of reach), give it a nudge to get it swinging and watch the little one follow its course.

## For the yummy mummies

# New mamas need treats, too!

The Indian mystic Osho once wrote that when a child is born a mother is too. What a comforting thought. We focus so much on how precious children are in every culture that it's easy to forget women themselves enter an entirely new phase of their lives during birth as well.

In India, when a new babe arrives, Mum is sent to bed for an entire month and not allowed to lift a finger. This is the one time in her life – even more so than when she's married – that a ceremony is put in place to treat her like a goddess. Her mother, friends and other family members cook all the food, give her daily massages and look after the little person between feeds. Her only job is to rest and feed her child, preserving the energy she needs for the months ahead. What bliss! An Indian friend living in Australia tells me she doesn't understand how some mums cope without the same support – she asked her own mother to fly over from India and stay for the year after her son was born, to provide her with as much help as possible.

In stark contrast, our society seems to put so much pressure on new mamas to appear in control and across the responsibilities of looking after a needy new bundle almost immediately. We are expected to welcome and entertain visitors before we've barely recovered from labour – let alone bonded with our child – and well-meaning friends and family are eager to meet and hold the new babe. Sometimes this feels like the last thing you want to do. Despite the incredible high of childbirth, hibernating in a cave with your newborn, partner and other children, if you have them, after the profound *rawness* of the entire experience seems preferable, but we're loath to admit it and often soldier on, almost out of politeness, rather than express this need.

With such a growing awareness of the corrosive and damaging effects of postnatal depression, everyone, it seems, is watching to make sure new mothers are 'coping'. How well I remember that feeling of needing to look together – even more so than I did before having a child – so people would think I was doing a good job (whatever that means). Friends remarked that I was a 'natural' mother, but this had the opposite effect of making me feel anxious not to disappoint. Their estimation was based purely on my appearance, which at times felt like a thin façade for the bone-tiredness and exhausting range of emotions I was feeling. This sense of high surveillance, coupled with the pressure in some circles to have an intervention-free birth experience, to breastfeed for as long as possible and to be an 'attached' parent, goes some way to explain why the first few months are the most rewarding, yet most challenging times a parent will ever experience.

It's gorgeous to give new parents something for their beautiful babes, but we should all endeavour to share some focus with mothers themselves. Because you can be certain they are looking out at this brave new world they have found themselves in with eyes as fresh as a newborn's. Let's treat them with love and support (softly, softly – save those horror stories for later if you must share them at all!) and give them all the time they need to adjust to their new role. And give them one of the following thoughtful treats to help them along the way.

# Nappy bags go incognito

Baby and fashion magazines with maternity features will tell you a nappy bag is the most important purchase for a new mama. As with clothes and equipment, it's wise to get organised early, but a specialist nappy bag, with all the bells and whistles, can set you back a small fortune. They also come in a limited range of styles and fabrics. Once the baby arrives, you realise all you really need is a largeish bag with comfy straps, rather than the trendy nappy bag *du jour* sported by all those celebrity mums.

Make this individual bag from your favourite fabric – upholstery material is good and hardy for a nappy bag. You want something big enough to hold nappies, a portable change mat, insulated bottle holder, wallet, keys, sunglasses, phone and other bits and pieces, but not so big that you'll be tempted to carry more than you need around in it. Add the baby and that's a serious load for your back to be dealing with. Even if you plan to only use it with the stroller, you don't want it hanging too heavy from the handles. Otherwise it might tip over (baby included) and you don't even want to think about that!

## Tip

If you have enough fabric, stitch a couple of pockets to the lining before sewing the bag together. This saves rummaging for little things, like dummies and keys.

# You will need

- 0.7 m x 112 cm-wide ($^3/_4$ yd x 44 in) sturdy upholstery fabric
- Same amount of cotton fabric, for your lining
- 0.6 m x 15 mm-wide ($^2/_3$ yd x $^5/_8$ in) ribbon
- Dressmaker's scissors
- Sewing machine and thread
- Measuring tape or ruler
- Iron
- Pins

# *Instructions*

1. Measure and cut two rectangles, each 55 cm (21$^1$/$_2$ in) square, from your upholstery fabric – this is for the outside of your bag.

2. Cut a strap approximately 80 x 10 cm (31$^1$/$_2$ x 4 in) from the same fabric.

3. Take your cotton lining and repeat Steps 1 and 2.

4. With rights sides together and allowing 1 cm ($^3$/$_8$ in) seams, stitch the outer bag sections together around three sides, leaving the upper edge open.

5. To create boxed corners, fold the lower corner into a point so that the side seam is centred at the apex and aligned with the bottom seam. Measure 6 cm (2$^1$/$_2$ in) down the seam from the apex and rule a straight line across the corner at this point. Sew across the ruled line, securing the stitching firmly at each end. Make another line of stitching close to the first for strength. Fold corner under bottom seam.

6. Repeat Step 5 for the opposite corner.

7. Repeat Steps 4–7 with the lining fabric, but leave a 20 cm (8 in) opening in one side seam during Step 4.

8. With *wrong* sides together, lay the two strap sections together. Using your iron, press under 1 cm ($^3$/$_8$ in) on each long edge (turning over both layers of fabric at the same time), then press under another 1 cm ($^3$/$_8$ in), making a neat double hem. Sew the hems in place, stitching close to the inner edge.

9. Turn the outer bag right side out. With right sides together, position and pin the ends of your strap to each side seam of the bag, allowing 6 cm (2$^1$/$_2$ in) on each end of the strap to extend above the raw edge of the bag. Machine-baste the straps in position.

10. Cut the ribbon into two 30 cm (12 in) pieces and cut one end of each piece on an angle.

11. Measure and mark the centre point on each opening edge of the bag and pin the raw ends of the ribbons to these points on the outside of the bag, with raw edges matching. Machine-baste the ends in place.

12. Slip the lining bag over the outer bag, so that the right side of the lining is facing the right side of the bag. Make sure your side seams and upper opening edges are aligned.

13. Allowing a 1 cm ($^3$/$_8$ in) seam, sew right around the upper opening edge, sandwiching the straps and ribbons in the seam as you stitch.

14. Now turn the whole thing right side out through the hole that you left in the lining side seam – how clever is that? Turn under the raw edges on each side of the opening and stitch the opening closed by hand or machine. Push the lining down into the bag.

15. Now topstitch around the upper edge of the bag, stitching 3 mm ($^1$/$_8$ in) from the edge.

16. Finally, to reinforce the straps, topstitch in a 5 cm (2 in) square on top of where the strap is inserted into the bag, stitching through all layers and stitching diagonally in both directions across the square for extra strength. (You can also do a smaller version of this over the inserted ribbon ends as well, if you like.)

# Day-nap eye patch

The most common piece of advice new mamas receive is 'sleep when the baby sleeps'. I guess this is because babies are such unpredictable little creatures, the one thing you can rely on is utter exhaustion and the need to catch up on sleep whenever (and sometimes wherever) possible.

My friend Ella, a mother of three, told me that when her first two children were small and her husband arrived home from work, she would literally collapse on the floor wherever she'd been standing and fall into a deep sleep. This will not come as a surprise for mums with babes who sleep badly during the night.

Napping during the day is essential while your baby becomes accustomed to the difference between night and day, and especially during that first, shattering month at home. Make this charming light-blocking eye patch for yourself or another mother in need of some shut-eye.

## You will need

- Approximately 25 x 15 cm (10 x 6 in) dark, thick fabric
- The same amount pale silk fabric
- Approximately 0.4 m x 20 mm-wide (16 x ³/₄ in) elastic – or enough to fit head size
- Dressmaker's chalk
- Embroidery needle and thread
- Sewing machine and thread
- Pure wool stuffing
- Dressmaker's scissors
- Pins
- Sewing needle and thread

## Instructions

1. Cut your dark, thick fabric into the shape on page 263 and repeat with the silk.

2. Use chalk to draw on eyelids and lashes on the right side of the dark piece, then embroider over the chalk with a contrasting thread before dusting off.

3. Lay both pieces of fabric together, right sides facing each other.

4. Position the elastic between the two fabric pieces with the elastic ends extending slightly at each side and pin together. Make sure that the elastic is not twisted and that the extending ends lie flat on each side.

5. Allowing a 6 mm (¹/₄ in) seam, sew over the ends of the elastic to secure it in place, reversing back and forth a few times for strength.

6. Now sew around the outside of the shapes, leaving a small opening of about 5 cm (2 in) where the top of the brow sits, and taking care not to catch the loop of elastic in the seam.

7. Turn the mask right side out through the opening.

8. Stuff the mask with a little wool stuffing – just enough to make it a little plump, but allowing it to still lie flat.

9. Turn in the raw edges of the opening and topstitch around the entire edge of the mask 3 mm (¹/₈ in) from the edge.

# Zippered purses

You really can't have too many nice zippered purses for holding all sorts of things. For a new mama, this can mean anything from spare change to makeup, tissues, dummies or painkillers.

These cute plastic-covered purses last forever, protect the things in your bag from scratches and small spills and pop easily inside a handbag. They can also be made to fit almost any purpose. Make a number of them at once and put aside for last-minute gifts. Or create a matching set in different sizes for weekends away and to display prettily on open shelves in the bathroom.

## You will need

- Two 22 x 17 cm (8³/₄ x 6³/₄ in) pieces clear plastic ( the kind used to protect an outdoor table)
- Two 22 x 17 cm (8³/₄ x 6³/₄ in) pieces upholstery fabric
- 20 cm (8 in) zip
- Sewing machine and thread
- Ruler

## Instructions

1. Place a piece of plastic on top of the right side of a fabric rectangle, aligning the edges. Repeat for the second pair.

2. With right side of zip facing right side (that is, plastic side) of one pair of rectangles, sew one side of the zip to the 22 cm (8³/₄ in) edge, using the zipper foot on your machine.

3. Repeat Step 2 for the second side of the zip and remaining pair of rectangles.

4. Open the zip by about 2.5 cm (1 in), then fold the fabric/plastic rectangles together so the plastic layers are on the inside facing each other. The edges on all four pieces should be lined up.

5. Allowing a 1 cm (³/₈ in) seam, sew around the remaining three edges, reversing a couple of times where the side seams meet the ends of the zip.

6. To create boxed corners, fold the lower corner into a point so that the side seam is centred at the apex and aligned with the bottom seam. Measure about 1.5–2 cm (⁵/₈ –⁷/₈ in) down the seam from the apex and rule a straight line across the corner at this point. Sew across the ruled line, securing the stitching firmly at each end. Make another line of stitching close to the first for strength. Trim off the corner.

7. Repeat Step 6 for the opposite corner.

8. Open the zip, turn inside out so the plastic is on the outside, and your purse is finished.

## Tip

✿ It can be a bit fiddly juggling two layers when you're sewing. If you're having trouble, try using oilcloth instead. (Modern oilcloth is a plasticised fabric, rather than the old-fashioned variety, which was actually impregnated with oil.) It is sturdy and waterproof but has the advantage of being only one layer. UK designer Cath Kidston stocks the most beautiful, high quality range I've seen.

# Fab feeding pillow

A good feeding pillow is pretty essential for a new mother – this tortellini-shaped number (made from an old souvenir tablecloth) sits in the lap and supports both elbows and baby, relieving some of the strain on a breastfeeding mother's arms and neck. Even using bottles, this pillow will make a difference as it helps prop *petits bébés* at just the right height for a feed.

## *You will need*

- ◉ Large piece paper (newspaper is fine) and a pencil
- ◉ Two 70 x 60 cm (27$^1$/$_2$ x 23$^1$/$_2$ in) pieces of fabric: go for pretty patterned cotton on top and plain denim or canvas underneath
- ◉ Dressmaker's chalk
- ◉ Dressmaker's scissors
- ◉ Sewing machine and thread
- ◉ Large bag pure wool stuffing
- ◉ Needle and thread

## *Instructions*

1. Use the pencil to draw the shape on page 264 onto the paper and add 1 cm ($^3$/$_8$ in) extra all round for seam allowance. Cut this out for your pattern.

2. Pin your two fabric pieces together, right sides facing each other, and place them on a flat surface.

3. Pin the pattern on top of the layers and trace around the outline with chalk.

4. Cut around the outline, through both layers, creating two matching shapes.

5. With right sides together and allowing a 1 cm ($^3$/$_8$ in) seam, sew around the outside edge, stopping 10 cm (4 in) before you get back to the starting point.

6. Sew around the outside again, very close to the first line of stitching to strengthen the seam. The pillow will be stuffed quite full with wool and used to support the weight of a baby, so you don't want the seams pulling apart.

7. Taking care not to cut through the stitching, use your scissors to snip across the seam allowance at 1 cm ($^3$/$_8$ in) intervals around the outer curves and in the tight inner curve.

8. Turn the pillowcase right side out through the opening.

9. Stuff the case with wool until it's completely full and plump.

10. Turn under the raw edges on each side of the opening and use your needle and thread to sew it closed with small strong stitches. *Bon appétit!*

# Stylish baby sling

In many countries, wearing babes in a sling is a way of life for the vast majority of women. It also makes breastfeeding mothers feel less exposed in public if they can master the art of feeding on the sly.

I have four slings in a range of fabrics to wear with different outfits. Apart from it being quite wonderful to wear a babe tucked against your chest, an early childhood centre nurse assured me that slings are the best way to carry a baby: they promote natural spine development and are also great for bonding with your wee one. Babes can curl up in a position they're most comfortable in (they'll certainly let you know if they're not) and you can get about your day while rocking them to sleep at the same time, hands free.

Just be careful not to hurt your back or neck – once babies get too heavy, gently lever them out and into the cot or pram. They might even stay asleep a bit longer if you're extra careful.

## You will need

- 60 x 150 cm (23$^1$/$_2$ x 60 in) upholstery fabric
- Sewing machine and thread (use a sturdy cotton thread and denim needle)
- Pinking shears
- Iron
- Measuring tape
- Dressmaker's chalk
- Ruler

**Tip**

A nice, soft alternative for a newborn is to make the sling from a cotton jersey fabric. The stretch makes it easy to hold the baby close to your body.

## *Instructions*

1. Fold your fabric in half crosswise so it measures 60 x 75 cm (23$^1$/$_2$ x 30 in).

2. Allowing 1.5 cm ($^5$/$_8$ in) seams, sew the 60 cm (23$^1$/$_2$ in) edges together, then stitch again, very close to the first line of stitching, for an extra-strong seam.

3. Use your pinking shears to neaten the edges of the seam allowance to prevent fraying, then press the seam allowance to one side. You now have a tube.

4. Using the iron, press under 1 cm ($^3$/$_8$ in) around one raw edge of the tube, then press under another 1.5 cm ($^5$/$_8$ in), and stitch this hem in place close to the inner pressed edge.

5. Hem the remaining raw edge of the tube in the same way.

6. Fold the tube in half lengthwise, bringing right sides together and matching hemmed edges.

7. Starting at the folded edge, measure inwards along the seam about 10 cm (4 in) and make a mark with your chalk.

8. Rule a 25 cm (10 in) straight line from the mark down to the folded edge of the sling on both sides, creating a triangle shape, with your mark at the apex.

9. Stitch along the ruled lines through both layers of fabric, creating a cradle shape at the bottom of the sling. Stitch again close to the original stitching lines for extra strength. There is no need to cut off the excess fabric in the triangle.

10. Turn the sling right side out, then pop *bébé* in for a rockin' good time.

*Forget the plane —*
*enjoy the holidays in your own home*

# summer

The meaning of summer has changed so much over the years, but to me it remains a season of childish pleasures. Think of the deliciousness of an icy-pole or quick dip on a hot summer's day, the joy of gatherings with friends and family, favourite tunes providing the soundtrack. Sand between the toes and the freedom of time outdoors in minimal clothing, basking in the lush heat of a long, lazy holiday. The same things that were all gorgeous way back when we were young are even more so now, because we realise how rare and precious these moments really are.

When I was little, my brothers and I usually got kicked out of the house from dawn to dusk to play in the garden, a nearby park or at the local pool. This gave us plenty of opportunity to hang out with the other kids in our street, building cubbies, riding our bikes and making up elaborate games that sometimes ended in a trip to Casualty. Broken bones aside, it was great fun, and I still remember those long summer holidays that seemed like heaven after the drawn-out agony of school. We worry so much more now about the dangers involved in letting kids out of our sight – certainly more than parents did in the '70s. I know all the reasons why, but I still feel nostalgic for a time when children had more freedom to come and go as they pleased.

As a teenager, summer became all about parties, camping and blowing off steam after the year of study – usually somewhere coastal and preferably with a music festival slotted in somewhere in the middle. My friends and I ran wild, but somehow, in the enviable way of teenagers, left ourselves with enough energy to face the year ahead refreshed.

I hung on to an enthusiasm for music festivals in my twenties, but then mainly looked forward to chill-out time on a beach somewhere, either in Australia or Asia, and relished spending time in accommodation far nicer than my own, which was invariably rented with a bunch of grotty flatmates.

Nowadays, and more especially since I became a parent, I'm much less inclined to spend summer somewhere less comfortable than my own house, which means I rarely go away at this time of year. It's not perfect by any means (a pool would make it so) but I love enjoying our home while the days are long – there's a steaminess to the air and things become decidedly more languid. Lazy time indoors is a fine thing. And one thing is certain: I no longer feel like hopping in the car or on a plane for a long-haul trip.

I can see the years ahead already, filled with garden parties, time outdoors and a paddling pool. I will bake more, and drive less. And make more things for friends, family and myself. And I will not stop indulging in the same things that inspire me to behave with childish enthusiasm, an essential quality that we should all work hard to retain along the way.

*If we took a holiday*

## Glamour both pool side and bar side

The easiest fashion decision is to pair strappy sandals with a floaty dress in summer. There's something effortlessly chic about the look because there is simply no need to go overboard on accessories. Coco Chanel once stated that a woman should always remove one item she is wearing before leaving the house (in this respect, I'm pretty sure she meant accessories rather than an essential item of clothing ...) Whatever is 'in' at the time, I keep coming back to this, the best piece of fashion advice I've ever heard. She also said that luxury must be comfortable, otherwise it is not luxury – what a seer Coco was, amid the opulence of turn-of-the-century Paris.

I love vibrant colour and interesting fashion pieces that convey something essential about the wearer, but I think fussiness is a fashion mistake too many women make. It always has the effect of making us look like we're trying too hard. And garish labels create the opposite effect than they're meant to by looking cheap, unless worn with an ample dash of irony. Even worse is wearing a number of labels on display at the same time – *quelle horreur!*

It took me years to work out my own fashion rules. Namely, make the effort to look your best every day, because the day you do skip the grooming regime is the day you're destined to run into someone important (or an ex-boyfriend). If you're the low-maintenance type, wear versatile outfits which will take you from day to night with a few simple accessory alterations. One standout item in an outfit is usually enough, and if you want to end up with a coherent- (rather than random-) looking wardrobe, you should probably think about what you already own when you buy something new, and make sure you have other pieces to wear with it. (The last is advice I aspire to, rather than heed.)

Take inspiration from the current trends but don't follow them slavishly. Spend more on good staple items and less on current-season

fripperies. Team voluminous tops with streamlined skirts or pants, or vice versa – don't wear tight or baggy clothes from head to toe. Avoid high-necked tops if you have a large bust, and emphasise a tiny waist with a cinched belt. Aim for clothes that can be dressed up or down; a vintage dress that looks equally good with flats or heels, say, or jeans smart enough to wear to work, a club or the park on the weekend.

The following easy pieces will always jazz up a simple outfit. Find one you like and make it in a variety of fabrics and colours, or collect pieces of fabric you know would flatter a friend and make one for her next birthday. And enjoy looking cool as a cucumber as you swish your way from one event to another, appropriate accessory worn *just so*.

# Elegant clutch

One of the best ways to dress up an outfit for an evening look is to ditch the larger, work-day handbag for a cute clutch or purse. Even if you haven't had a chance to pop home for a shower and a change, switching to a smaller clutch will make you seem like you did. How much does one really need when out on the town, anyway? Cash, cards, keys, lipstick and phone should be enough and, with careful editing, these should all fit in the one small bag.

You can afford to be inventive with fabric when going for such a small accessory to your look – play with tooled leather, velvet or bold vintage prints, and team with a gorgeous button and the finest silk or cotton to create a pretty, contrasted lining.

## You will need

- 43 x 32 cm (17 x 12½ in) fabric, for outer bag
- Same amount pretty contrast fabric, for lining
- A great-looking, large button
- Measuring tape
- Needle and thread
- Sewing machine and thread
- Dressmaker's scissors
- Iron
- Press stud

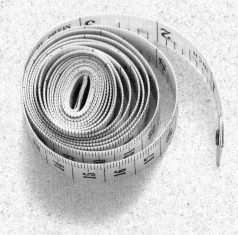

## Instructions

1. Lay your two rectangles of fabric together, right sides facing each other. Use a dinner plate to trace a curved edge onto the two top corners. Trim along your traced curve – this will be the flap.

2. Take your outer bag piece and, with the right side facing you, measure about 5 cm (2 in) in from the centre top edge of the flap and sew on your button with needle and thread.

3. Lay your bag pieces back together, with right sides facing each other and edges aligned.

4. Allowing a 1 cm (³/8 in) seam, sew around the outer edges, leaving a 10 cm (4 in) opening in the middle of the shorter straight edge.

5. Trim away the seam allowance diagonally on the corners and carefully clip across the seam allowance at 1–2 cm (³/8–³/4 in) intervals around the curves, taking care not to cut your stitching.

6. Turn the bag right out and press thoroughly with your iron. Turn under the raw edge on each side of the opening and press again.

7. Topstitch right across the short end of the bag, near the edge – this will close your opening at the same time.

8. Lay the bag on a flat surface with the lining facing upwards and the flap at the top. Measure up 15 cm (6 in) from the bottom straight edge on each side of the bag and mark with a pin on each side. Fold up the bottom edge of the bag at this mark, bringing wrong sides together, and pin at the sides – it should look like an envelope, with the button on the outside of the flap.

9. Topstitch the side edges of the bag together: start at one bottom edge and sew up the side, about 3 mm (¹/8 in) from the edge, reversing a couple of times for reinforcement when you get to the opening edge, then continue around the flap till you get to the opening edge on the other side, reinforce as before, then finish sewing the second side.

10. Sew the top part of your press stud to the inside of the flap, directly under the button. Fold down the flap to see where you should place the other half of the stud, then sew it in place on the outside of the bag. Happy dancing.

# Bold beach bag

*Leave the phone at home for a change, and don't forget a big umbrella!*

## You will need

- 0.7 m x 112 cm-wide ($^3/_4$ yd x 44 in) sturdy upholstery fabric: I'm not usually a fan of acid brights but this is the time to go all out if you want to – lurid colours look great on the beach
- The same amount of contrasting fabric for your lining (here I've used a pretty oilcloth, because it's waterproof)
- Large decorative button (optional)
- Measuring tape
- Dressmaker's chalk
- Dressmaker's scissors
- Sewing machine and thread
- Ruler
- Iron
- Pins

It's a good idea to keep a beach bag packed in the boot of your car in the summer months for last-minute dashes to escape the heat. That way you don't need to head home first, or you can leave immediately while the sun is shining and arrive before it disappears.

Don't forget to take the following essentials:
- A new fashion magazine or trashy novel
- Towel
- Bikini or swimming costume
- 30+ sunscreen
- Spare change for an icy pole and cold bottle of water

## Tip

Oilcloth is a good lining because it's waterproof, but if you're using a fabric lining instead, you can sew the strap in place on the bag so that the right side of the strap is against the wrong side of the bag.

# *Instructions*

1. Measure and cut two 50 cm (20 in) squares of upholstery fabric. Lay the squares together, right sides facing each other, and use a dinner plate to trace a rounded edge onto the two lower corners. Trim along your traced line, through both layers.

2. Use one of these pieces as a pattern to cut two matching lining pieces.

3. From both the outer fabric and the lining fabric, cut a strip, 10 x 80 cm (4 x 31$^1/2$ in), for the strap.

4. From a scrap of upholstery fabric, cut an 18 cm (7 in) square, for the inner pocket.

5. With right sides together and allowing a 1 cm ($^3/8$ in) seam, stitch the two outer bag sections together around the sides and bottom, leaving the upper straight edge open.

6. On the outside of one side of the bag, measure down about 10 cm (4 in) from the centre of the top straight edge and stitch a decorative button in place, if you like.

7. Using your iron, press under 1 cm ($^3/8$ in) on each edge of the inner pocket square, then press under another 1 cm ($^3/8$ in) on one edge only and stitch this double hem in place close to the inner edge.

8. On the right side of one lining piece, measure down 11 cm (4$^1/4$ in) from the centre of the top straight edge. Position the hemmed edge of the inner pocket at this point and pin in place. Sew the pocket to the lining around the three pressed edges, leaving the upper hemmed edge open and reinforcing your stitching at the upper edge on each side.

9.  With right sides together and allowing a 1 cm ($^3$/8 in) seam, stitch the two lining bag sections together around the sides and bottom, leaving the upper straight edge open.

10. Slip the lining bag into the outer bag so that the wrong sides are facing each other and the side seams and upper edges are aligned.

11. Turn under 1 cm ($^3$/8 in) on the upper raw edge (turning under both layers of fabric at the same time), then turn under another 1.5 cm ($^5$/8 in) and stitch this double hem in place, close to the inner edge.

12. With *wrong* sides facing each other, lay the two strap sections together. Turn under 1 cm ($^3$/8 in) on each short end (turning over both layers of fabric at the same time), and stitch across to secure. Now turn under 1 cm ($^3$/8 in) on each long edge, then press under another 1 cm ($^3$/8 in), making a neat double hem. Sew hems in place, stitching close to the inner edge.

13. With the lining side of your strap facing the lining of the bag (so that when you carry the bag on your shoulder, the fabric rather than the oilcloth is against your skin; see Tip on page 95), position the ends of your strap over the side seams of the bag, placing the bottom of each strap about 6 cm ($2^1$/2 in) below the hemmed edge.

14. Stitch the straps in place, stitching in a square around the end of the strap and reinforcing the stitching by sewing across the two diagonals as well.

15. Load up your beach bag essentials and head to the beach.

# D-ring and Obi belts

## You will need

- Strips of pretty fabric and/or ribbons – use any style you like and experiment with different fabrics. If you are using something delicate like silk, pair with a sturdier piece of cotton or canvas for your backing.
- 2 D-rings (the size will depend on the width of your belt)
- Ribbon or woven cotton tape, for tying the Obi belt
- Contrasting ribbon (optional)
- Measuring tape
- Dressmaker's scissors
- Pins
- Sewing machine and thread
- Iron
- Chopstick
- Sewing needle and thread (optional)

## Tip

For super-quick D-ring belts, use a length of 25–30 mm-wide (1–1$^1$/$_4$ in) pretty striped or spotted grosgrain ribbon and simply stitch one end to your D-rings and either fuse or snip the other end at an angle to prevent fraying. Easy!

D-rings are the D-shaped metal buckles found most commonly on men's cloth belts, and Obis are those wide bands used to cinch the waist of traditional Japanese kimonos. Wear a D-ring belt looped through the top of hipsters or cinched loosely around your middle, and a wider Obi to really draw attention to your waist.

Think of these striking belts as wearable art. Paired cleverly with a plain dress, they can bring an entire look together or completely transform a simple outfit into something spectacular.

The following cloth belts are the perfect way to use a divine length of ribbon or small, gorgeous strips or pieces of fabric you've collected on your travels. Make them with the $150 per metre Liberty print you have been saving forever and been too scared to use, or the remains salvaged from a favourite vintage number.

## Instructions: D-Ring belt

1. Use the tape measure to measure the widest part of your hips, then add 15 cm (6 in).

2. For a finished belt 5 cm (2 in) wide and the right length for you, cut two strips, each 7 cm (2³/₄ in) wide by the above measurement. This takes into account a seam allowance of 1 cm (³/₈ in).

3. Decorate one of the strips with a beautiful contrasting ribbon, if you like.

4. Pin the strips right sides together. Trim one short end of the strips diagonally at 45 degrees, to create a neat pointed end.

5. Allowing a 1 cm (³/₈ in) seam, stitch around the edges of the strips, leaving the straight short end open.

6. Carefully trim away the seam allowance on the corners of the pointed end, but don't cut too close to the stitching.

7. Turn the belt right side out, gently pushing a chopstick into the corners on the pointed end to turn them out neatly. Press the belt thoroughly.

8. Turn under the seam allowance on the raw edges of the open end and press again.

9. Thread the open short end of the fabric strip over the straight edge of the two D-rings and stitch the end in place across the width of the belt, reversing at each end of the seam to secure the edges firmly.

# *Instructions*: *Obi belt*

1. Use the tape measure to measure around your waist, adding 4 cm (1$^1$/$_2$ in).

2. For a finished belt about 12 cm (4$^3$/$_4$ in) wide, cut two strips, each 14 cm (5$^1$/$_2$ in) wide by the above measurement. This takes into account a seam allowance of 1 cm ($^3$/$_8$ in).

3. With right sides together and allowing a 1 cm ($^3$/$_8$ in) seam, stitch the two pieces together around the edge, leaving one short end open.

4. Trim the corners to reduce bulk, then turn the belt right side out, gently pushing out the corners with a chopstick, and press.

5. Turn under the seam allowance on the raw edges of the open end and press again.

6. Stitch the opening edges together neatly by hand or machine.

7. Take two pieces of ribbon about 60–80 cm (24–30 in) longer than the belt and sew in a straight line around the middle of the belt about 5 cm (2 in) apart. If the ribbon looks lovely against the fabric, you can wear it on the outside. If you want to keep the belt simple, you will only need four pieces of ribbon, measuring 30–40 cm (12–16 in) each, sewn beneath the short edges of your Obi belt.

8. Tie in a bow at the back of your outfit.

# Apron top

Fling one of these on over jeans and a t-shirt, or a simple dress for a very cute look. Think of it less as a top than an accessory, and enjoy the flounce of criss-crossed ribbons trailing at the back and striking covered buttons up front.

## You will need

- Second-hand men's shirt, or about 60 cm (24 in) square fabric – a light denim works really well
- 25 mm-wide (1 in) bias binding in a contrasting colour
- 3.5 m (3¾ yd) ribbon, at least 1 cm (³/8 in) wide
- 2 large, covered buttons or button badges, for decoration
- Dressmaker's scissors
- Large piece scrap paper
- Ruler and pencil
- Pins
- Sewing machine and thread
- Needle and thread

## Instructions

1. Take your men's shirt and cut away the back section along the seams, up to the yoke seam across the shoulders. This will give you a flat piece of fabric.

2. Using the diagram on page 262, rule up a pattern on scrap paper and cut it out.

3. Pin the pattern to the fabric and cut it out – there's no need to add seam allowance as you are going to bind the edges.

4. Hold the fabric shape up against yourself in the mirror, and pinch darts into the sides to fit around the bust area.

5. Sew the first dart into place as pinned. Adjust the second dart so that it exactly matches the size and position of the first dart. You can sew the darts by bringing the right sides together and stitching on the wrong side, or you can topstitch the darts in place, working on the right side of the fabric.

6. Press your bias binding in half along the length, wrong sides together.

7. Slip the raw edge of your apron shape between the folded edges of the binding and stitch the binding around the edge, easing gently around the curves and reversing a few times at the end for strength.

8. Cut two 5 cm (2 in) lengths of ribbon and fold over to make loops.

9. Sew a loop into place on each side at the back of the apron, with the loops sticking out directly beneath your arms.

10. Cut the remaining ribbon in half.

11. Sew one end of the remaining ribbon lengths to the back of the top edge of the apron on each side. Take the ribbons diagonally across each other and thread them through the side loops.

12. Make sure you have enough ribbon to tie in a bow at the back in the centre and then cut off any excess ribbon at an angle.

13. Place the covered buttons at the front of the top, moving them until you are happy with their position, then sew them firmly in place with needle and thread.

# Customised tee

I've always liked tongue-in-cheek slogan t-shirts. They're a bit rock 'n' roll, casually chic, and a popular MOD (model off-duty) look, too.

These individual tees look great under a denim jacket or blazer, with jeans or a pair of shorts or simply oversized and on their own for the beach: just cut away the round neck and sleeve hems to complete the look. They make a great gift for a boyfriend, girlfriend, baby or child, and the possibilities for coming up with creative ideas to make new ones, year after year, are endless.

## You will need

- Soft cotton t-shirt
- Iron-on printer paper (from office supplies stores)
- Computer and printer
- Your own image: this can be a photo or scan of anything, from fabric or wrapping paper to a magazine page (but remember that words will print back-to-front unless your copier will copy in reverse)
- Paper scissors
- Iron

## Instructions

There should be detailed instructions on the back of the iron-on paper pack, but basically you will need to scan your image, print it out on the iron-on paper, cut around the outside, line up on the front and centre of your tee and iron flat.

# Dress renovation

*Here are some simple ideas for transforming old, tired dresses into a signature outfit*

◎ Take up the hemline to the most flattering spot on your leg. For me, this is just above the knee: a good length for showing off thin calves, but generous enough to hide the saddlebags I've been carrying about on my thighs for the past few years. Remember to fold the fabric over and sew the hem by hand if it isn't too bulky, as you might want to let it down later.

◎ Use a belt to cinch in the waist. This is a particularly good solution for updating '80s drop-waist numbers and to emphasise a '50s full skirt.

◎ Remove gridiron-player shoulder pads, letting the loose fabric fall naturally over your real shape or popping in a few stitches to tailor it.

◎ Cut a new neckline. I've made a decision to get rid of everything I own that is high-necked: it's taken me forever to admit that they just don't suit me. You might think you're working the Audrey Hepburn look, when in reality all that extra fabric is making you look like a matronly barrel.

◎ Shorten sleeves. For some lucky ladies, cap sleeves look very cute. If you're more reticent about showing untoned upper arms, try a three-quarter-length sleeve.

◎ Change the buttons. An easy solution, but very effective for bringing an old item bang up to date. Don't forget to take frocks with you when you shop for new buttons and be bold: give yourself the time to check a whole variety of shapes and colours and you might be surprised by what works best.

◎ Add chic jewellery, like a fab brooch or bangles worn clinking up the arms.

◎ Pair a loud frock with incredibly simple makeup, hair and accessories. An '80s body con sheath that screamed 'look at me' back then can be toned down to sleek and sexy with a pair of nude sandals, a clean face and a simple chignon.

Apart from washing neighbours' cars at the heady rate of $3 each, my first job in my early teens was at a florist. I was paid $40 a week to turn up for a few hours every day after school and on Saturdays to wash out the slimy flower buckets with bleach. Glamorous, I know. But $40 seemed to stretch a long way back then, and I felt like the richest girl I knew.

This is when I started trawling op-shops for second-hand clothes to renovate. Armed with the latest issue of *Dolly* or *The Face* magazine for inspiration, I bought musty-smelling men's tweed coats and corduroy pants from the Salvation Army store, pairing them with a white singlet and decorated lapels, or a '40s tea dress with the hemline drastically cut and chunky Doc Martens. Think Molly Ringwald in *Pretty In Pink*, with about as many hits and misses. This was my first real foray into recycling.

I have always loved playing with fashion but have never really had the money for designer labels and to satisfy my desire to wear something new every day. The few pieces I have purchased full-price were credit-card blowouts I paid for (and usually regretted) later; the rest come from sample and end-of-season sales. But, by and large, the majority of my wardrobe is made up of market and charity store finds. It's Murphy's Law that my cheapest pieces are the most treasured, such as the $50 black ball gown from the '40s which weighs a tonne, fits like a glove and makes me feel like Grace Kelly in *To Catch a Thief*. Or the cream beaded cashmere cardigan, paltry price forgotten, still in immaculate condition at least 70 years after it was first made.

Developing an eye for quality fabrics and styles that suit you is incredibly valuable, as it will save you both a great deal of time and money over the years.

*Open house*

## Sumptuous party decorations

There's nothing better than attending a great party. You know the ones: where everything just works, even if it doesn't go according to plan, and everyone is caught up in a kind of manic, magic buzz. Even better is when you're the host and you have yourself to thank for putting on such a memorable event.

I love dinner parties, morning and afternoon tea parties, barbecues and breakfasts. Cocktails. Christmas Eve drinks. Any occasion where friends will be present, I'm usually there and in the thick of things. Life feels a bit flat without a party to look forward to.

Spoil your guests rotten by making a special drink for the day and naming it in their honour. Bake up a storm, or decorate the house especially. Children's birthday parties are a great excuse to go all out with bunting, strings of paper dolls, creatively iced biscuits, cupcakes and themed costumes.

Get into the spirit of holidays like Christmas by making personalised gift stockings, tree decorations and edible gifts for guests to take home, wrapped simply in calico and tied with a gorgeous ribbon. Place enticing gifts under the tree or decorated branch in a delicious pile.

And send handmade invitations and thank you cards, because courtesies like this are not so common anymore. Not only will it be appreciated, but it might inspire people to start doing the same thing more often in return.

# Gorgeous party bunting

Bunting is very simple to make and makes any occasion look so fun and festive. When I was living in London, the Queen celebrated her Golden Jubilee after 50 years as the reigning monarch. At the time, it seemed that everywhere you looked were strings of red, white and blue bunting decorating shopfronts and homes, which were also plastered with the Union Jack. This was surprising, really, when not so many people would consider themselves monarchists anymore. I think the Brits were just looking for an excuse to fly the flag and get into a party spirit.

Keep bunting in your cupboard to decorate the house, front fence or backyard on the eve of a special occasion. Or pin it up all year round in a child's room to make every day a cause for celebration.

## You will need

- About 3 m x 112 cm-wide (3¹/₄ yd x 44 in) cotton fabric in total, in at least two different colours or prints (to make a string of 20 bunting triangles)
- About 8 m x 20 mm-wide (8²/₃ yd x ⁷/₈ in) ribbon or cotton tape (you want to have lots of ribbon free on the ends to suspend bunting from trees, gates or walls)
- Scrap paper and pencil
- Ruler
- Dressmaker's scissors
- Pins
- Sewing machine and thread
- Iron
- Safety pin

# *Instructions*

1. On scrap paper, rule a triangle measuring 25 cm (10 in) across the base and 25 cm (10 in) tall from base to apex. Cut this shape out and use it for your pattern.

2. Use the pattern as a guide to cut out 40 triangles in total, taking care not to waste any fabric along the way by flipping the triangle around and using the previously cut line as the edge of the next triangle.

3. When you have finished cutting out your triangles, pair them up with right sides together.

4. On each pair, put a pin or make a mark on each side seam, about 3 cm (1¼ in) up from the base of the triangle. Then put another pin or make another mark about 3 cm (1¼ in) further up from the first mark.

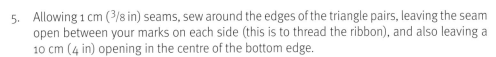

5.  Allowing 1 cm ($^3/_8$ in) seams, sew around the edges of the triangle pairs, leaving the seam open between your marks on each side (this is to thread the ribbon), and also leaving a 10 cm (4 in) opening in the centre of the bottom edge.

6.  Trim off the seam allowance on each of the points and turn each triangle right side out.

7.  Turn under the seam allowance on the raw edges of the opening on the bottom edge and topstitch across the opening to close the seam.

8.  Press the triangles thoroughly.

9.  Attach the safety pin to one end of your ribbon or cotton tape. Thread the safety pin and tape through the opening in one side of a triangle, taking it across between the layers of fabric and out the opposite opening. Pull the ribbon through until you have about 1 m (39 in) left extending from the left-hand edge.

10. Topstitch back and forth across the opening on both sides to secure the bunting triangle in place on the ribbon.

11. Now take the safety pin and tape through the next bunting triangle in the same way until you have about 10–12 cm ($4–4^1/_2$ in) of tape between triangles. Stitch the bunting in place, as before.

12. Repeat Step 11 until you have threaded all the triangles onto the tape, leaving the excess tape extending at the right-hand edge.

13. Affix the bunting with drawing pins or tie the ribbon ends to backyard trees, and enjoy watching the triangles shift and snap in the breeze.

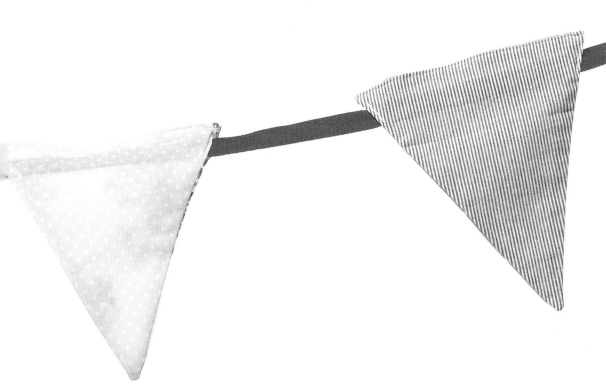

# Paper dolls

Just as with origami, a few small steps can turn a simple piece of paper into an art form. Or at least, a very satisfying chain of paper dolls to be hung along the walls.

The work of UK artist Robert Ryan has received international fame over the last few years. His beautiful, poetic pieces and book *This is for You* strike a chord with so many people. He has inspired me to experiment again with the childish pleasures of paper, scissors and glue. And unless you do so already, after a few hours spent doing just this, you will come to understand the popularity of scrapbooking.

## You will need

- A roll of crépe paper (from a newsagent or stationery store)
- Pencil
- A sharp set of paper scissors

## Instructions

1. Remove crépe paper from its packaging but leave it in its rolled-up shape.

2. Draw the outline of a simple person, with arms outstretched to reach both sides of the paper roll.

3. Use scissors to cut around the outline, making sure you don't cut around the hands at the folded edges, so that each person remains linked to the next one by the hands.

4. Repeat this process with the remainder of the roll, experimenting with various shapes – making sure that each shape is linked at the fold on each side of the roll.

5. Unroll the paper to admire your entire string of dolls in mirror image.

# Pinwheels in the wind

## You will need

- Paper card (from craft stores, newsagents or scrapbooking supplies)
- Ruler
- Pencil
- Paper scissors
- Drawing pin and mapping pin
- A dowel stick around 30 cm (12 in) long — the best are thin plant stakes, from nurseries or stores selling gardening supplies

## Instructions

1. Use your ruler and pencil to rule a square onto your paper. It can be any size you like — but about 20 cm (8 in) square is a good size. Rule diagonal lines across the square from corner to corner in both directions.

2. Cut along each diagonal line about two-thirds of the way to the centre of the square, dividing each corner into two points.

3. Fold alternate points into the centre, one after the other so that the points overlap.

4. Push a drawing pin into the centre point through each of the layers and wiggle it around to make the hole a little loose around the pin — this will enable the pinwheel to turn more freely.

5. Remove the drawing pin, then push a mapping pin through the hole to attach the wheel firmly to your stick, and start blowing. The pinwheel should spin effortlessly in a good gust of wind.

I haven't been to a fair day in years, but aren't pinwheels so evocative of childhood visits to the Royal Easter Show and annual school fetes? You can almost smell the fairy floss just by looking at them.

Make a stack of pinwheels in a basket for a small child's birthday party and watch them marvel at the everyday miracle of paper turning in the wind. And don't forget to make each one from the same materials to avoid arguments!

## Tip

* The double-sided cardstock that scrapbookers use is perfect for these pinwheels, but you can also use spray adhesive to glue two pretty papers together. If you're having trouble getting the wheel to spin, make sure your pin is not pushed in too tightly. You can also thread a small metal or cardboard washer or even a small bead onto the pin to keep things loose.

# Personalised gift stockings

Christmas has never been a big thing for me in the past, but I've really come to love decorating the house for the holiday season and marking the day as different from any other in the year. My resolution is to celebrate it every year in future, and play host to any 'orphan' friends who aren't able to spend it with their own families.

Honour friends with an invitation to Christmas lunch and make them feel welcome by creating a gift stocking with their name on it. Even if your family doesn't know the extra guests personally, ask them to bring small gifts that anyone would appreciate, such as an elegant bar of soap, or chocolates, so the non-family members feel included in all the festivities.

## You will need

- Remnants of old jumpers and/or sturdy upholstery fabric – don't feel you have to stick to red, white and green, but using at least a little red or green will make them unmistakably 'Christmassy'
- Ribbon
- Dressmaker's chalk
- Dressmaker's scissors
- Embroidery needle and thread
- Sewing machine and thread
- Needle and thread

# *Instructions*

1. Lay out your remnants and find two pieces large enough to draw a generous boot or sock shape on.

2. Find two contrasting strips of fabric, which can be used for the cuff on the stocking.

3. Take your chalk and draw the outline of a boot (or sock) onto the wrong side of your first piece of fabric (don't forget to allow extra for seam allowance all round), then cut it out.

4. Use this as a pattern for your second piece, laying and pinning the fabrics right sides together before cutting.

5. Cut two contrasting cuff strips to fit along the top of each stocking.

6. With right sides together, sew a cuff to the top of each stocking shape.

7. Before you sew the stocking shapes together, take your chalk again and write your guest's name on the front of the stocking. You could also draw a small motif such as a snowflake or star somewhere on the stocking – but remember to allow for the seams and don't go right to the raw edge.

8. Use your embroidery needle and thread to embroider the name and motif.

9. Take your ribbon and sew in a line across the cuff. You might want to do this with the embroidery needle and thread in large stitches of a contrasting shade.

10. With right sides together, and matching cuff seams, sew the stockings together around the outside edge, leaving the top edge open. Zigzag along the raw edges of the seam allowance if you think your fabric is going to fray badly.

11. Snip carefully across the seam allowance at 1–2 cm ($^3/_8$–$^3/_4$ in) intervals on the curves, taking care not to cut the stitching, and then turn the stocking right side out.

12. Fold in the raw edges at the top in a single or double hem and topstitch around the edge to secure.

13. Take another short piece of ribbon, fold into a loop with the ends together and sew the ends inside the opening of the stocking.

14. Pin stockings to the underside of a wooden mantelpiece, or loop through with string and hang to hooks on a picture rail above your Christmas tree.

*Tip*

Make a few stockings with a simple Christmas motif, such as a star, instead of a name. These can then be used as gifts for unexpected guests.

# Tree decoration

Although lush-looking and tasteful, the best Christmas trees are not those perfectly colour-coordinated versions you see in department stores every year. I far prefer the more organic kind, boasting a collection of bought and handmade baubles, ribbons, tinsel, stars and angels collected by a family over the years. Think outside the cookie-cutter for a more modern and personal take on tree decoration.

Your 'tree' could be an old branch simply adorned with red and white ribbon. Or wire hung from a hook in the ceiling and embellished with ornaments on pegs and twine. It could also be the traditional pine, hung with a mish-mash of your child's most cleverly constructed decorations, lovingly stored year after year.

Don't buy into a retailer's vision of Christmas – it's so much nicer to create your own traditions based on family members' favourite things and personal tastes.

*Some suggestions for amassing your own collection of beautiful tree decorations*

◎ Encourage children to make at least one piece a year, out of anything they like. It could be painted plaster, plastic or loo rolls – present them with a range of materials and persuade them to go wild. Praise them for their artistic skills and when Christmas is over, ask them to help deconstruct the tree and choose their favourites. Wrap in tissue paper and store somewhere safe and dry for the following year.

◎ Trawl the stores during the post-Christmas sales for one or two divine glass or hand-painted ornaments, prices slashed, and store for next Christmas.

◎ Collect favourite ribbons from gifts throughout the year and use to tie bows to the ends of each branch.

◎ If you're not doing presents this year or you're donating the money you would normally spend to charity, ask guests to bring an ornament for the tree instead. This will be easy and inexpensive for them to do, and the decorations will remind you of favourite people you shared Christmas with for years to come.

# Edible gifts

## For each person you will need

- A good-sized portion of banana bread – enough for say, 4 slices
- A sheet of baking paper
- Large square of calico or patterned fabric
- A gorgeous length of ribbon
- Packing label, pen and twine for your card

## Instructions

1. Bake your banana bread (cookies and other baked goodies also work well for this gift) and allow it to cool completely.

2. Wrap in baking paper, and then in the fabric.

3. Hold all the sides of the fabric up together, then tie ribbon around and into a perfect bow.

4. Write the recipient's name and any birthday or Christmas wishes on the packing label, then loop twine through the hole and tie underneath the bow.

It is one thing to make something for friends that they can keep, but another to give something appealing to their tastebuds instead, that is instantly satisfying. I love my food, so I really appreciate it when my host presses boxed leftovers on me after a special gathering, or I receive the gift of a specially chosen hamper of gourmet foodstuffs. Here, I've added edible goodies to this collection of other handmade gifts, so you can remember that cooking for someone is always another option.

Last Christmas I was really struggling with what to give my male friends. In the end, I decided on a small loaf each of home-cooked banana bread, made to my favourite recipe.

*Paint it black*

# Breathtakingly simple furniture restoration

To my mind there's nothing more stylish or comfortable than a home lovingly furnished with appealing, eclectic pieces that have been acquired over time. Trinkets picked up on foreign holidays, handmade anything, the occasional ultra-modern designer piece saved up for and bought, and items scoured from auction houses – all fleshed out with flea market finds and an affordable storage solution or two from IKEA.

Design magazines are a great source of inspiration, but there's something soulless about re-creating an entire look for your own home. It's the household equivalent of wearing a designer's catwalk look from head to toe: completely uninventive. Homes should reflect the personality of their inhabitants, and provide a space for them to be surrounded by pieces that 'speak' to them. This is unlikely to happen when an interior designer chooses everything, or you fill the house after one trip to a homewares megastore. Building a beautiful environment takes time.

To this end, you should always be on the lookout for pieces that grab you. A consideration of how they'll fit in with the rest of your belongings helps, but I honestly believe that if you only buy the things you love, you can't go wrong. It might not be to everyone's taste, but you will always look forward to coming home, and be guaranteed to get a kick out of your living environment every single day. What could be more grounding than that, after a day spent staring at a computer monitor in a grey cubicle?

You don't need a massive budget to buy beautiful furniture. Second-hand and antiques stores are overflowing with used pieces that, given a few simple alterations, will look like new again, or at least lovingly distressed. Consider the following questions when trawling the stores: Can I paint it? Can I strip and wax it? Can I line it with beautiful paper? Even chipped wood veneers can be salvaged with a lick of paint. Turn a fault into a feature by highlighting it and dressing up the rest. Take an old trunk with chipped edges, peeling stickers and rusty handles; these look beautiful as is, strewn with a few gorgeous hardcover books and a stylish lamp.

Keep your eyes open — what are the pieces nobody wants, and why? Fashions are always ebbing and flowing like the tides, so work out what you like about certain eras of furniture, and see how you can refurbish or update even the most outdated styles. Mid-century Scandinavian furniture, which was all the rage when it originally came out but went through a prolonged period of unpopularity, is now hip again – pieces you could pick up for a pittance only ten years ago are now flying out the door of second-hand shops for thousands. If you like a piece of furniture but it looks tired or outdated, think about what you could do to make it stylish again – re-upholstering, painting, or stripping and staining. Use your initiative and you'll be amazed at how thrift store furniture can come alive again, and save you a small fortune in the process.

*Paint it white*

# Milk painting

Milk paint is a traditional wash favoured in French country antiques, and usually comes in pastel or earthy shades. It takes time and many coats of application to complete, but the finish is gorgeous and unique. Made from – yes – milk, it has a delightful chalky texture which softens the look of just about any wood, and acts as a beautiful backdrop to ceramics and textiles.

For many months after moving into our home, I agonised over whether to install built-in wardrobes in the bedrooms. I've never really liked the way they look, but they're so useful and I was finding it difficult to source stand-alones in the right size or look for our Victorian-era cottage. After lots of hunting, I realised my favourite pieces were French antiques – very shabby chic, big enough to fit all our clothes and shoes, but well out of our price range.

I began visiting local auction houses hoping to find a bargain, but was quickly outbid by professional dealers who knew the demand was high. I soon realised that the pieces that didn't sell, or went for much less, were the heavier, darker wardrobes I associated with men's clubs and grandfather clocks. In beautiful woods, like walnut or cedar, they had the quality I was looking for but not the visual appeal.

I finally found a tall, wide cedar robe, which was simple but boasted a few beautiful features like claw-and-ball feet and carved flowers and curlicues on the doors. It had been passed in at auction several times after not making the owner's reserve. I managed to buy it for a very reasonable sum but when it arrived, it was so dark and overwhelming. I hated how imposing it looked in our bedroom – it seemed to shrink the size of the room. I soon set about stripping and milk-painting it, finishing with a delicious-smelling beeswax. It's now one of my favourite items of furniture in the house.

# Decorative lining for chests and drawers

## Tip

Good storage is important in any home, but particularly in houses with children. Built-in cupboards and robes are expensive and worse, permanent. Free-standing furniture or shelving that uses storage boxes and containers as a feature is far more adaptable and interesting. Think laterally about what you can use to store items you use frequently or less so: re-use anything from an old tin to woven baskets or brightly coloured fruit boxes.

## You will need

- An old wooden trunk or chest
- Wallpaper to fit the sides of its interior
- Measuring tape
- Light sandpaper and wooden block
- Scissors
- Craft glue

## Instructions

1. Measure your chest to work out how much paper you will need to cover all the interior surfaces, except for the inside lid (or maybe including the lid too, depending on the design of the trunk). Do this by measuring the inside height and width of one of the shorter sides and multiplying by two. Measure one of the longer sides as well and multiply by three – this should give you your complete measurements.

2. Rip or scrape out any old paper in the chest if appropriate, making the interior surface as smooth as possible. If the wood is bare, use a sheet of light sandpaper wrapped around a wooden block to make it smooth.

3. Cut the wallpaper to fit within each inside edge.

4. Use craft glue to stick paper to each side.

5. Leave open to dry for a few days before it is ready to use again as storage for board games, winter clothes, bed linen or anything else you are not currently using.

As with the decorative lining on a coat or suit, beautiful lining in chests and drawers is a fun way to inject personality into your furniture without making it look like it's screaming for attention.

Wallpaper and interior decorating stores often sell paper remnants. The internet is also a great place to source discontinued lines or vintage wallpaper from an earlier era.

*Keep them busy*

# Things to make for and with children

I think I had to have children – there are simply too many enjoyable things from childhood that I want to indulge in again, and having children is the perfect excuse for revisiting them. Such as games, or playing for hours in dress-up clothes. Living with a dog and waterslides. Messy painting and crafts projects, licking the bowl, fancy dress parties, and reading.

I can't forget the wonder of discovering favourite children's authors for the first time; Enid Blyton, Dr. Seuss, C.S. Lewis and Roald Dahl. Classics such as *The Hobbit*, Lucy Maud Montgomery's *Anne of Green Gables*, Madeleine L'Engle's *A Wrinkle in Time* and Maurice Sendak's *Where the Wild Things Are*. I'm almost jealous of the little ones who haven't read them yet, because the discovery of finding those words you will love for the first time is so delicious, it's a minor miracle. I look forward to introducing Olive to new books which have become modern classics since I was a child – the Harry Potter books, and Philip Pullman's *His Dark Materials* trilogy. And maybe I'll give her the first adult's book I ever read (and loved) when she's old enough: John Irving's *A Prayer for Owen Meany*.

Then again, she may not be interested in reading. She may not want to lick the bowl, or learn to sew. But I will encourage her to seek out her own happiness.

I'm no Stepford Wife, but over the last few years I've been itching to collect and make the best dress-up costumes, and bake from a book of decorative birthday cakes. To host inspired children's parties and festoon the yard with coloured ribbons, strings of cut-out dolls and paper lanterns shifting in the breeze, letting the kids eat cake and playing pass-the-parcel and pin the tail on the donkey with them in childish abandon.

I do hope that we can give our daughter a creative upbringing. One that continues to nourish and inspire her long into her adult life. I want to encourage her to engage with all forms of artistic expression, but more importantly, I want to help her to realise she can make anything she wants to, anything at all – from writing a book to designing clothes or filmmaking, to cooking; or from painting high art to decorating a room.

Making this link is vital. Too often we are impressed by things and assume someone far more talented than us created them. And it's within the interests of a great deal of people for this fiction to exist. I'm still annoyed that it took me years to work this out for myself.

If there's anything I want to teach her, it's that she really can do (almost) anything. Surely that is the desire of every parent?

Most kids adore dressing up, and they couldn't care less whether clothes fit properly or not. Often it's a thrill to simply try on grown-up things and pretend to be someone else. Buy them an old chest or suitcase for their bedroom and start collecting things for fancy dress outfits to inspire the imagination. Read them favourite fairytales and ask them which character they want to be.

The best costumes are all about the accessories: collect old beads, glasses, wigs, stage makeup and crazy shoes for kids to clomp about in. Forget about the hire shop – it's easy enough to create your own. Use the following checklists for three easy children's outfits, sourcing what you can from your own wardrobe, the local charity store and a two-dollar shop. Help children construct any missing accessories from cardboard, paint, scissors, staplers and glue.

# Clothes for the dress-up box

*Pirate* — inspired by Long John Silver or Captain Hook in *Peter Pan*

- ◎ Striped shirt
- ◎ Eye patch
- ◎ Red or black bandanna
- ◎ Sword
- ◎ Gold earring
- ◎ Blackened tooth

*Fairy princess* — à la Tinkerbell (also in *Peter Pan*)

- ◎ Floaty slip or dress
- ◎ Wings
- ◎ Wand
- ◎ Silver glitter, sprinkled liberally

*Cowboy/Cowgirl* — from true tales of America's Wild West era

- ◎ Hat
- ◎ Western-style shirt
- ◎ Denim jeans
- ◎ Boots with spurs
- ◎ Gunbelt and toy gun
- ◎ Pony (just kidding)

# Creative cupcake decoration

## You will need

- Cupcake or muffin mix (or create your own from scratch using a favourite recipe. I'm a sucker for Nigella Lawson's cupcake recipes in *How to be a Domestic Goddess*)
- Cupcake papers
- Cupcake baking pan
- Icing sugar
- Food dyes in a variety of colours
- Piping bag and decorative nozzle
- Cake decorations: silver sugar balls, hundreds and thousands, Smarties, licorice and jellybeans offer myriad decorative possibilities

## Instructions

1. Preheat the oven to the temperature specified in the recipe.

2. Put the cupcake papers in the holes in the cupcake pan.

3. Let the kids help with measuring and mixing up the cake batter, then fill the papers almost to the top.

4. Pop the tray in the oven to cook, removing to cool when done.

5. Mix up at least two colours of icing with sugar, food dye, lemon juice and water to make the right consistency.

6. When the cupcakes have cooled down, smooth icing over the tops with a spatula, and put the other icing mixture into your piping bag with a nozzle to create more intricate designs, such as stars or writing.

7. Let the kids go bananas with the decorations.

8. Scoff cupcakes with the kids and, if at all possible, put some aside for them to take to school the following day.

Children thrive when given the freedom to be creative. A dress-up box is one way to unleash their imagination; another is giving them free rein in the kitchen. Cooking is the perfect way to indulge childish creative expression – particularly when it comes to baking sweet treats.

Little girls have long been the recipients of dolls and miniature versions of everyday domestic appliances pertaining to cooking and cleaning, while boys are usually given dinosaurs, trucks and building blocks. Attend any child's birthday party and when the time comes to open the gifts you'll see this is still the case. At least there's one place where the traditional gender stereotypes are being addressed: many kitchenware shops now sell both pink and blue mini-aprons, cookie cutters and utensil sets to encourage all kids to go wild in the kitchen.

Help little ones enjoy spending time in the heart of the home by familiarising them with everything it contains from an early age. Explain the dangers of a hot stove and boiling water but don't make them fear everything (true in the kitchen, as in life!). A great piece of parenting advice I once read recommended leaving one kitchen cupboard free from child-proofing and filling it with wooden spoons, sturdy pots and pans and other safe utensils for them to play with and bang together. And as with the rest of their toys, rotate them often so they don't get bored.

When children are older, let them enjoy themselves preparing food. This is a great way to overcome problems with fussy eaters. Even a ham and cheese sandwich can be fun to make with a judicious squeeze of mustard or tomato sauce for a smiley face. Let kids mix cake ingredients together and go a little easy on scolding them about floury or sugary mess. And allow them to lick the spoon and bowl when you're finished – that's half the fun.

## Devilish delights

Years ago, when I was living in Melbourne, a friend held an exhibition at a gallery to showcase his sons' art, with the sales proceeds going to a local charity. They were four and five respectively – it sold out. The boys were virtually bouncing off the walls (in a good way), and I thought it was a special and unique gift from their father, giving them confidence in their creative ability and an early understanding that there are lots of ways to be involved in charity.

Over the past few years, I've received quite a few cards and artworks made by friends' children. What a brilliant idea. Asking a child to create something special to say thank you, or as a gift, teaches them generosity and consideration from a young age. It's also a positive way for them to receive attention.

You need very little equipment to start kids off on their own artistic projects: provide paper, paint, scissors and glue and you're a good way there. Here are some ideas to get them going.

# *Rorschach paintings*

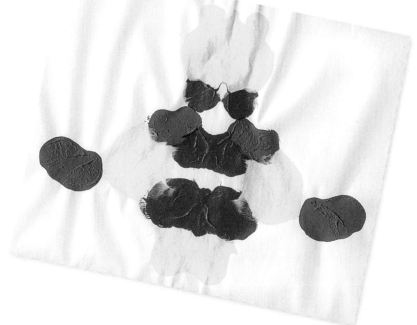

## *You will need*

- ◉ Blank A4 (letter size) paper
- ◉ Non-toxic acrylic paint

## *Instructions*

1. Fold a piece of A4 (letter size) paper in half, then open and lay flat.

2. On one side of the fold, paint a few blotches in different colours. Squish both sides of the paper together and open it up again.

3. Have fun asking kids to explain what they see in the resulting images: a butterfly, a bat, a face. Start worrying only if their answer to each one is an axe murderer.

You know the scene from any number of Hollywood films: tortured protagonist sits in therapist's chair while said therapist holds up flash cards with inkblots, asking what he sees in the murky images. Those images are Rorschach paintings, developed by Herman Rorschach in 1921 as a (questionable) means of psychological evaluation. They always look like butterlies to me... I'm not sure what that says about my psyche.

# Colour bubbles

**Tip**

I wouldn't attempt this inside, as you're all going to get very messy, but kids will love this. Get them kitted out in a painting smock or apron first, and make sure they're not wearing their Sunday best outfits underneath.

## You will need

- Wire coathanger or other firm wire
- Pliers
- Butcher's paper
- Non-toxic acrylic paint
- Dishwashing detergent

## Instructions

1. Take a pair of pliers and cut the bottom, straight edge off a wire coat hanger.

2. Bend one end around to make a circle and twist the ends closed.

3. Tack up some butcher's paper on a wall outside, and fill a few empty jam jars with a small amount of water, some bright paint and dishwashing detergent.

4. Dip the wire circle into one of the jam jars then blow a bubble through the circle directly on to the paper. Keep going with different colours until you've created a rainbow of colourful splats.

5. When the paint dries, cut the paper up to be used as wrapping paper, thank you cards or a poster for the bedroom wall.

# Collages

The beauty of a collage is that you can use pretty much anything — paper, fabric, buttons, leaves, wood — to make up a finished image, so they are a wonderful way to recycle. Collect small, bright fripperies in a tin when you come across them. Bottle tops, sequins and ribbons are particularly useful for collages, as are old magazines, foil chocolate wrappers or greeting cards.

## You will need

- Canvas or cardboard
- Old magazines or newspapers
- Safety scissors
- Random found objects
- Non-toxic craft glue

## Instructions

1. Set the kids up with a canvas or piece of cardboard and help them draw an outline of something instantly recognisable: an elephant, a bird or even an abstract circle or other shape if your child seems to be more of a modernist.

2. Tell them to stick away to their heart's content, using images cut or torn from magazines and any of the found objects that take their fancy.

# Fabulous felt fripperies

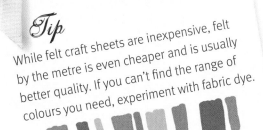

## Tip

While felt craft sheets are inexpensive, felt by the metre is even cheaper and is usually better quality. If you can't find the range of colours you need, experiment with fabric dye.

## You will need

- Sheets of felt in all the colours of the rainbow to allow a tiny person's imagination to soar
- Dressmaker's chalk
- Dressmaker's scissors
- Needle and embroidery thread
- Scraps of wool
- Craft glue
- Cardboard
- Sticky-backed magnets
- Brooch pins
- Fibrefill or wool stuffing

Felt is plentiful and cheap and is a great material for simple craft projects. It's malleable, doesn't fray, wears extremely well and can be sewn or stuck together with glue. Buy A4-sized sheets of felt from a haberdashery or crafts store and pop them in the kids' craft cabinet for making things such as soft toys, jewellery, three-dimensional cards and magnets for the fridge.

## Instructions: Fridge magnets

1. Use dressmaker's chalk to draw an outline of any shape directly onto felt, then cut around it with scissors. Flower and simple animal shapes work well; and so do geometric shapes, such as squares, triangles or circles.

2. Decorate with thread, buttons, sequins and other felt shapes, such as letters, either sewn or glued in place.

3. To reinforce the shape, you can glue it to cardboard, if you like.

4. Apply a sticky-backed magnet to the back for a cool piece to decorate the fridge.

## Instructions: Doll

1. Cut out two simple outlines of a person.

2. Decorate the face and add any other features that you like, such as clothing.

3. Place the two pieces together, wrong sides facing, and sew around the outside with embroidery thread or wool in a contrasting colour.

4. Leave a small space for stuffing and then sew the opening closed.

5. Add some woollen hair, if you like.

## Instructions: Brooches

1. Cut a flower shape out of brightly coloured felt and then a smaller circle in a contrasting colour to sew in the centre.

2. Sew on a brooch pin for a cute piece of jewellery.

# Papier mâché

## You will need

- Chicken wire in a small cross-hatch, usually available from a hardware store or garden nursery
- Tin snips
- Wallpaper adhesive, mixed with the amount of water listed in the instructions on the back of the pack
- Newspaper, ripped into long thin strips
- Acrylic paint and paintbrush

## Instructions

1. For a head, construct a big round ball out of chicken wire with a flat base, attaching an extra cylinder to the area where the nose should be – this could be made of chicken wire as well or even an empty toilet roll. Create a depression for the eyes and mouth, and curve some cheeks into the face.

2. Rip an old newspaper into strips, and dip strips in a bowl filled with a mixture of powdered wallpaper adhesive and water. Layer the strips over your wire frame, and leave to dry. Wait a few days (weeks or months work too!) then come back to the sculpture to apply extra layers. When you're finally finished and the paper is all dry, paint facial features and hair onto the head, experimenting with different expressions: sad, angry, happy.

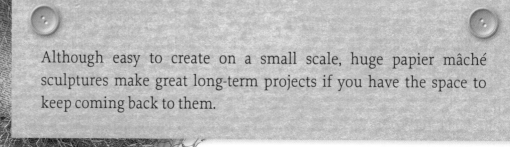

Although easy to create on a small scale, huge papier mâché sculptures make great long-term projects if you have the space to keep coming back to them.

# Tepee

I really wish I'd had one of these myself when I was younger because, far and above, my favourite childhood game on a rainy day was transforming our living room sofa into a cubby house, using sheets and broom handles to construct a hideaway den. It was a sad time indeed when it had to be dismantled and turned back into a sofa at the end of the day.

I'm convinced that preoccupying every minute of our children's time leads to their suffering from much shorter attention spans as adults. All kids need a special space to escape to for some time with their own imagination. A place to read, write, play games and dream. Or just to sit and enjoy some time quietly contemplating things, *sans* grown-ups.

Set this tepee up in the corner of a child's room or in the backyard on a sunny day. Let them drag whichever toys and games they like inside and check on them occasionally, perhaps to offer snacks like strawberries with cream or fairy bread. Encourage time without TV or video games and long stretches of imaginative play.

## *You will need*

- ◉ 1.5 m x 112 cm-wide (1²/₃ yd x 44 in) *each* of three contrasting fabrics, for the outside of the tepee (you will have some fabric left over for smaller projects, but you need this amount unless you plan to patchwork)
- ◉ 7.5 m x 112 cm-wide (8¹/₄ yd x 44 in) calico, for the lining
- ◉ 5.2 m x 25 mm-wide (5²/₃ yd x 1 in) fairly sturdy ribbon or woven cotton tape (lovely, bright, striped grosgrain is great, if you can get it)
- ◉ Four 1.8 m x 25 mm-diameter (70 in x 1 in) wooden dowels, from a hardware store
- ◉ Measuring tape
- ◉ Ruler
- ◉ Dressmaker's chalk
- ◉ Scissors
- ◉ Bobble-headed pins
- ◉ Sewing machine and thread
- ◉ Iron
- ◉ Needle and thread

# Instructions

1. Lay calico out on the floor or a large table, and use your tape, ruler and chalk to measure and draw a triangle that is 90 cm (35$^1$/$_2$ in) across the base and 140 cm (55 in) high from base to apex.

2. Cut out the triangle with your scissors.

3. Fold down the apex until the top folded edge measures 15 cm (6 in) from side to side. Press the fold line with your fingers to mark it, then open out the fabric again and cut off the top of the triangle along the marked line. The shape you now have is a triangle with the top lopped off – a bit like a volcano.

4. Use this piece as a pattern to cut four more 'volcano' pieces from calico, and one 'volcano' piece from *each* of your coloured fabrics – eight pieces in all, including your original pattern piece (four calico pieces for the lining, and three coloured and one calico piece for the outer tepee).

5. Measure halfway down the side edges of four of the calico triangles and make a small mark at this point.

6. Cut four 70 cm (28 in) lengths from your piece of ribbon and fold each piece in half crosswise. Trim the cut ends at a neat angle to prevent fraying.

7. With right sides together, pin two of your calico triangles together along one side edge, matching your halfway marks. Slip the folded end of one of your ribbons in between the layers at the marked point, so that the folded end extends about 1 cm ($^3$/$_8$ in) beyond the raw edges and the angled ends lie between the calico sides. Pin in place.

8. Allowing a 1.5 cm ($^5$/$_8$ in) seam, stitch the sides together from top to bottom, sandwiching the folded end of the ribbon in the seam and reversing back and forth over the ribbon a couple of times for extra strength.

9. Press the seam allowance open (snipping through the extending fold on the ribbon) and stitch down each side, about 12 mm ($^1$/$_2$ in) from the seam. This will make the seams sit flat upon the dowel.

10. Following Steps 7–9, add the three remaining calico triangles, one after another, sandwiching a folded ribbon between each seam. When you've sewed all four triangles together, you should have a funnel-shaped tube.

11. Take hold of one of the triangles in the tube and fold it in half lengthwise, aligning the seamed edges. Press along the fold with your fingers to mark the centre line. Open it out again and cut along the centre line, from top to bottom – this is to create the opening flaps in the tepee.

12. Using your iron, press under 1 cm ($^3$/$_8$ in) on each raw edge on the flaps, then press under another 1 cm ($^3$/$_8$ in) and stitch this double hem in place close to the inner edge.

13. Press under 1 cm ($^3$/$_8$ in) around the upper raw edge, then press under another 1 cm ($^3$/$_8$ in) and stitch this double hem in place.

14. Finally, press under and stitch a double hem around the lower edge.

15. Repeat Steps 7–14 for the outer layer of the tepee, omitting the ribbon ties in the seams.

16. Cut four 35 cm (14 in) lengths of ribbon and trim one end on each into an angle.

17. From the top, measure 40 cm (16 in) down the opening edge on each outer flap and mark with a pin. Measure 30 cm (12 in) further down from this pin and mark with another pin.

18. Sew a ribbon tie at each pin mark, turning under the raw edge of the ribbon before you sew.

19. Place your two tepee layers together, wrong sides facing, and pin the upper edges together. Topstitch around the upper edge to secure.

20. Lap one edge of the flap over the other by about 5 cm (2 in) at the top and pin. Secure this opening by making a 4 cm (1¹/₂ in) square of stitching through all four layers, with reinforcing lines along both diagonals as well. Sew again on top of your first line of stitching, for extra strength.

21. Pin the lower edges of the tepee together, leaving the flap sections unpinned. Topstitch the edges together.

22. Set up your dowels by tying the remaining length of ribbon around all four, about 30 cm (12 in) from the top, securing all four pieces together.

23. Pull out the bottom 'legs' of the dowel to form the corners of a square, creating your tepee's frame, then lay the tepee over the frame, aligning the seams along the dowels.

24. Tie the lining ribbons to each dowel on the inside and adjust the legs until the fabric is neatly stretched over the frame.

25. Your tepee is finished – let your little ones know they can keep whatever toys they like inside and let them keep the inside as messy as they like. The front flaps will hide whatever they have strewn about, and this lets children savour their first, non-parentally organised space without driving mum *loco*.

*Tip*

❋ This is probably the trickiest project in this book, but only because it's the most time-consuming and so requires more patience and careful measuring to get the dimensions right. However, the tepee will look fantastic even if you are out by a few centimetres in different places.

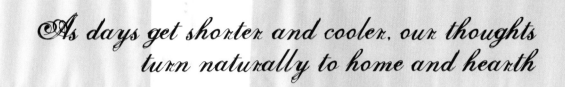

*As days get shorter and cooler, our thoughts turn naturally to home and hearth*

# autumn

Oh, how I love the crisp, sunny days of autumn! That early morning bite in the air that heralds the turning of the first leaf to russet – an excuse to swap sandals for long leather boots. After the exhausting heat of late summer, it's such a welcome relief, and I start to get very excited about the months ahead: pulling out clothes consigned to storage since the early days of spring, and packing away bikinis and floaty summer dresses with lots of lavender and clove sachets to ward off the moths. I do the same with bed linen and soft furnishings, changing cushions on the sofa, digging out warm throws, swapping the light summer duvet for a thicker, feather-filled version and using richer, darker-coloured pillowcases and sheets to make the bedroom less fresh and breezy, and more enticing.

Getting your wardrobe and home ready for the new season in this way gives you a fresh outlook and new perspective. It's an important act of revival and change, which is something we all need, to put a little spring in our steps. In countries like Sweden, where the shift in seasons is so much more extreme, people even go to the extent of swapping floor rugs, lampshades and artwork

to match their inner sanctums to the weather outside at different times of the year.

People usually stop going out as much once the days grow cooler. Inevitably, my thoughts turn to home and hearth – fewer cocktails at sunset and forgetting to eat; more red wine and cheese, perched at my kitchen bench as the nights become darker earlier. My projects become more about homely comforts like entertaining, interior decorating and rugging up. This is when I dig out the heavier fabrics, such as wool and velvet, which are too hot to really enjoy handling in the warmer months.

The longer evenings can be perfect for whiling away the hours painting or making collages, listening to old Dinah Washington recordings or even with the TV burbling away. And the kitchen becomes a focal point, where family and friends converge to eat and catch up on the day's news. We definitely find ourselves inviting people over more, as it's much more fun to cook than in a steamy kitchen in summer.

Relish the change in seasons and remember: it's almost as good as a holiday.

## The Crafty Minx in the kitchen

# Look heavenly stirring the pot

To my mind, the kitchen is the heart and soul of a home, where friends and family congregate for the most important activity of all – eating. Ours was built in the 1950s, so although it has some desirable fittings, such as sturdy plywood cupboards, it's quite dated compared to those in most other people's homes. We dream about renovating it at some stage, opening it up onto the backyard and giving ourselves more room for guests, but last autumn was when I decided to make it gorgeous now, or at least until we have the budget and energy for a proper overhaul.

Starkly whitewashed when we first moved in, I painted the cupboard doors in ice-cream colours of mint green, fairy floss pink, lemon yellow and duck egg blue, which look delicious contrasted against the white frames and black and white chequerboard linoleum on the floor. Because I was covering such small areas I only needed to buy 250 ml test pots of paint from the hardware store rather than entire litres of each colour. I've picked up on these colours with cheap and cheerful paper lanterns from Chinatown, which hang from underneath the wall units, and my beloved green vintage Formica dining table takes pride of place in the middle of the room. Crockery and cooking equipment are stored carefully around this small space for handy retrieval and ease of use. It's such a joy to be in.

I adore decoration and display, but not without purpose: what's the point of keeping out items that only work to gather dust and that horrible oily sheen peculiar to cooking areas? Kitchens should be living and breathing places that are constantly evolving, based on your needs.

Teapots and fine bone china cups and saucers are beautiful items to show off, and earn their keep if you drink as much tea as I do.

I've always yearned for a delicate set of china plates, the likes of which were once handed down in families for generations. My dear friend Katrina chose a divine set from Jasper Conran for Wedgwood on her wedding reception gift list – a clever move, as it will likely become an heirloom for her own family. My in-laws, keen collectors with impeccable taste, gave us elegant antique silverware instead, in a simple 'fiddle and thread' design. You can't always have everything you want, but there are ways to complement your finer belongings with thriftier purchases. The overall effect is so much more unique and personal than designer-everything anyway.

On my jaunts through charity shops and flea markets, I've found that there are literally thousands of gorgeous plates, cups and saucers out there – the sole remaining members of once-splendid sets. And because they no longer belong to their original families, they're usually very cheap to acquire. I have managed to amass a huge, harmonious collection for afternoon tea parties, and find the different colours, patterns and designs delightful to serve up and just to look at. You can follow a theme, such as a flower pattern or colour, or simply work them all together for a deliberate clashing effect, as I have.

Love your kitchen and it will love you back – food and the art of eating is not just about giving yourself the necessary fuel to get through the day. It's also about nourishment and, ultimately, satisfaction.

# 'Suzy Home-maker'
## '50s retro apron

These are one of my favourite things to pick over in flea markets. Unlike many other great finds from the '50s, there's still an abundance of frilly aprons available in striking fabrics and in fairly good condition, because not many people seem to wear them anymore.

Always one to jump at the chance for dressing up, I have a modest collection for baking days and afternoon tea parties. Coordinate your apron with the icing on your freshly baked hummingbird cake or store-bought marzipan biscuits. It's not purely practical, but not pointless either. Being a domestic goddess is less about slogging over a hot stove and more about style, anyway.

## You will need

- 80 x 40 cm (32 x 16 in) soft cotton in a pretty pattern (vintage '50s is ideal, so look for old tablecloths or damaged dresses from this era to cut up if you can't find the right fabric in a bolt)
- 1.5 m x 10 cm (1²/₃ yd x 4 in) plain fabric in a contrasting colour
- 2.5 cm-wide (1 in) bias binding to match plain fabric
- Dressmaker's chalk
- Dressmaker's scissors
- Iron
- Sewing machine and thread
- Measuring tape
- Pins
- Ruler

# Instructions

1. Fold your patterned fabric in half crosswise so it measures 40 cm (16 in) square. Using a dinner plate or something similar, trace a curve onto the outer bottom corner of the double fabric and cut along your traced line, through both layers, to create rounded edges on the bottom of your apron skirt. Open out the rectangle again.

2. Press the bias binding in half along its length, wrong sides together. Slip the raw edge of the apron skirt between the folded edges of the binding and use your machine to stitch the bias binding around the sides and bottom of the rectangle, taking care to ease it around the curved bottom edges.

3. Measure along the top raw edge of the apron and mark the centre point with a pin. Starting at this centre point, make a number of evenly spaced 1–2 cm ($^3$/8–$^7$/8 in) pleats across the top of the apron towards the side edge in one direction, then return to the centre point and make the same number of pleats towards the side edge in the other direction. Hold each pleat in place with a pin. When you have finished, your apron should measure about 40–44 cm (16–17$^1$/2 in) across the top edge – if it doesn't, adjust some of your pleats on each side of the centre point until it does.

4. Now machine-baste across the top edge, about 6 mm ($^1$/4 in) down from the raw edge, to hold all the pleats in position, removing the pins as you sew.

5. Fold your plain fabric waistband strip in half crosswise and mark the centre point of one long edge with a pin. Open out again.

6. With right sides together and raw edges even, pin the pleated apron to the marked long edge of the waistband strip, matching the marked centre points. Allowing a 1 cm ($^3$/8 in) seam, stitch the apron to the waistband as pinned.

7. Pull the skirt of the apron down over the seam and press it with your iron.

8. Now fold the waistband strip in half lengthwise on itself, bringing right sides together.

9. Use your ruler and scissors to trim both short ends of the folded waistband at an angle – this isn't absolutely necessary, but it looks pretty when finished.

10. Allowing a 1 cm ($^3$/8 in) seam, stitch across one short end of the waistband, pivot on the needle at the corner and stitch along the lower raw edges until you get to the edge of the skirt. Reverse-stitch a little to stop the seam unravelling. Repeat this process for the other end of the waistband.

11. Turn the waistband right side out, pushing out the angled corners with your fingers.

12. Turn under the remaining raw edge on the waistband and pin in place. Now topstitch right around the edge of the waistband, stitching close to all four edges. This closes the remaining part of the seam and gives a nice topstitched finish.

# Kitchen goddess high-waisted apron

## You will need

- Approximately 65 x 95 cm (25 x 37 in) reasonably stiff upholstery fabric in a rich design (the exact amount will depend on your height. The sides of the apron should wrap around your sides about halfway: mine measures 65 cm (25 in) across. The bottom hem should end about mid-calf.)
- 2 m x 20 mm-wide ($2^1/_4$ yd x $^7/_8$ in) ribbon
- Ruler
- Dressmaker's chalk
- Dressmaker's scissors
- Sewing machine and matching thread

Retro aprons in pastels and floral patterns are cute and playful in the manner of a '50s housewife, but sometimes it's good to amp up the glamour when you're throwing a dinner party. What would Audrey have worn while taking hors d'oeuvres out of the oven in her chic black cocktail dress, apart from a commanding presence?

This is an apron modelled on the long high-waisted kind that cocktail waiters wear – very flattering, particularly if you have a tiny waist. It should come just under your chest and tie in the front. You'll look like the hostess with the mostest, at ease in her own domain – simply pair with a winning smile.

Look for rich upholstery fabrics with patterns in raised velvet or a bold print. These will be sturdy enough to withstand any casserole splashes leaking through to your outfit beneath, and look finished enough to wear as an apron skirt even when you're not cooking. Simple ribbons wrapped around to tie at the front complete the look.

# Instructions

1. Hold the fabric up to yourself to work out how wide and long you want your apron. Take into account the pattern, making sure the most attractive section is centred in your middle. Make sure the shape of your fabric is a perfect rectangle – use a ruler and dressmaker's chalk before cutting to straighten up the lines.

2. Stitch a double hem on all four sides – that is, press under 1 cm (3/8 in), then press under another 1.5 cm (5/8 in), thus ensuring that all raw edges are completely concealed. Use the reverse button on your machine a few times at either end to secure stitching.

3. Cut about 15 cm (6 in) from your ribbon, fold it in half and trim the ends diagonally. On one inside upper corner of the apron, stitch the raw ends of the ribbon in place, creating a hanging loop.

4. Cut remaining ribbon in half, turn under one raw edge on each piece and attach a ribbon tie to each side of the apron, approximately 8 cm (3 in) down from the top edge. Sew back and forth over the attached ends a few times for sturdiness.

5. Trim the ribbon ends at an attractive diagonal angle to prevent fraying. They should hang down prettily when you wrap it around yourself and tie in a bow. *Voilà!*

# Oven mitts you'll want to wear outside

Maybe I'm looking in all the wrong places, but I've never found a really appealing pair of oven mitts in a shop. The fabric is usually too practical and boring, or features a naff print, like unpeeled onions and an orange hotpot. And the melt-free plastic versions are just plain ugly, even in hot pink.

I've made these from a very sturdy remnant of deckchair fabric. I love the Paul Smith-esque stripes in candy colours. Tough enough to handle the hottest dishes, they're also delicious to look at and should take pride of place on any kitchen hook.

## You will need (For each mitt)

- About 30 x 70 cm (12 x 28 in) quite sturdy upholstery fabric (deckchair fabric is perfect but any thick, durable canvas will do. Avoid synthetics as they tend to melt at high temperatures, or catch on fire ... very inappropriate)
- Same amount of calico for lining
- Same amount of old blanket, pure wool, felt or cotton quilt wadding
- 10 cm (4 in) narrow ribbon, for hanging loops
- Large piece scrap paper and pencil
- Dressmaker's scissors
- Dressmaker's chalk
- Pins
- Needle and thread
- Sewing machine and thread

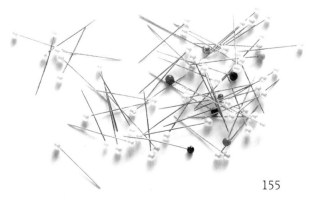

# *Instructions*

1. Lay your paper on a flat surface and place one hand flat in the centre. Keeping your fingers together and splaying out your thumb at a 90-degree angle, trace loosely around the outline of your hand to give a mitt shape.

2. Now add 5 cm (2 in) extra all around the traced line – it will look very big but you'll be surprised at how the extra allowance seems to be taken up and you don't want a tight glove. Cut out around the outer line – this is your pattern.

3. Cut the upholstery fabric in half crosswise, giving two pieces each 30 x 35 cm (6 x 14 in), and lay the pieces right sides together.

4. Pin the paper pattern on top of the fabric, trace around the outline with your chalk and cut out two mitt shapes.

5. Repeat Steps 4 and 5 for both the lining fabric and the blanket or wadding – you will have six mitts altogether.

6. Take your lining and blanket mitts and pin them together in pairs, with the blanket laid against the wrong side of the lining. Trim away 1.5 cm ($^5/8$ in) on the wrist edge of each of the blanket pieces – not the lining.

7. Using a needle and thread, tack the edges of each blanket/lining pair together to hold them secure.

8. With right sides together and allowing a 6 mm ($^1/4$ in) seam, sew the upholstery fabric mitts to each other around the edge, leaving the bottom (wrist) edge open.

9. Taking care not to cut your stitching, use your scissors to snip across the seam allowance on the curves and snip into the inner corner where the thumb section meets the hand. This will make the curves sit flat when the mitt is turned.

10. Turn under 1.5 cm ($^5/8$ in) on the raw wrist edge and press. Turn the mitt right side out.

11. Repeat Steps 8–10 for the blanket/lining mitt, but do not turn it right side out. Taking care not to snip into the stitching, trim the seam allowance back to 3 mm ($^1/8$ in).

12. Put the lining mitt onto your hand like a glove (the seams are all still on the outside), then push your gloved hand into the outer coloured mitt, like putting on a second glove over the first. All the seams are now on the inside, concealed between the two layers.

13. Fold your ribbon in half into a loop and slip the raw ends between the two wrist edges near the outer side seam. Pin it on the outside to hold.

14. Pin the pressed wrist edges together and sew around the edge with two rows of stitching – sew the first row right near the edge and the second about 5 mm ($^1/_4$ in) from the first.

15. Make a second mitt in the same way, if you wish. Since the mitt has the same fabric on both front and back, both right and left gloves are exactly the same.

# Artfully appliquéd tea towels

I seem to use tea towels a lot in my kitchen (and definitely more than I should as dust rags, sponges and oven mitts ...) so they tend to go in the wash every couple of days. I also prefer fabric in a pale cotton. Not surprisingly, they get dirty quite quickly.

This is my solution for covering burn holes and marks that you can't shift on tea towels that still have some life in them. Of course, they don't *need* to be stained to begin with and you can appliqué away to your heart's content if you simply like the way these look.

## You will need

- A cotton or linen tea towel
- Flowers, birds or other fabric images you like, preferably in a similar-weight cotton or linen to your tea towel
- Pinking shears
- Pins
- Sewing machine and thread or sewing needle and thread

## Instructions

1. Make sure your appliqué fabrics have been washed and dried before you use them, or you might find them shrunk or stretched out of shape after the first wash.

2. To prevent fraying, use your pinking shears to cut around the outsides of your fabric 'pictures', leaving about 6 mm (¼ in) extra around the outline, for stitching.

3. Line up the image over your tea towel where the stains are, and pin in place.

4. Using a needle and thread or the zigzag stitch on your machine in a contrasting colour, sew the image in place, reversing a couple of times at the end so it won't unravel.

5. Now admire your handiwork: you might find it looks too good for a tea towel and you'd like to frame it instead, which is another possibility ...

## *Tip*

✲  I prefer to sew my images by hand, but zigzag is
very quick. If you're not used to using the zigzag
on your machine, practise on scrap fabric first, and
experiment with the stitch length and width until
you get a stitch that looks nice and is wide enough
without puckering the fabric. If you're having trouble
keeping the appliqué image in place while you sew,
tack it in place first or use a dab of appliqué glue.

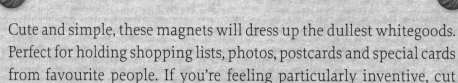

Cute and simple, these magnets will dress up the dullest whitegoods. Perfect for holding shopping lists, photos, postcards and special cards from favourite people. If you're feeling particularly inventive, cut different shapes into the fabric, such as birds and hearts.

# Fridge magnets

## You will need

- Floral patterned fabric
- Felt
- Pinking shears
- Sewing machine and thread
- Dressmaker's scissors
- Self-adhesive magnets – from crafts or stationery stores

## Instructions

1. Cut around the flowers on your fabric with pinking shears to give nice crinkly edges that won't fray.

2. Place a flower on a double layer of felt.

3. Set your sewing machine to the zigzag stitch and sew around the outside edges of the flower. A contrasting thread looks wonderful.

4. Using ordinary dressmaker's scissors, cut around the felt surrounding the flower, leaving a few millimetres around the outline to frame it.

5. Adhere your sticky-backed magnet on the wrong side, then place on fridge door.

## Tip

 If you get endless magnetised junk mail in your letterbox, pull off the magnets and use them for this project instead of buying them. You'll need a dab of craft glue to hold them in place but they work perfectly well and can be cut to the size you need.

## *The hostess with the mostest*

# Tempting tableware

For me, much of the pleasure to be had from eating well has to do with food presentation. The context in which it's served also makes all the difference to the taste. I relish nothing more than devouring fried fish and chips from yesterday's newspaper, buffeted by a salty wind on the beach; or green papaya salad on a plastic plate from a street stall in Thailand; but eating directly out of takeaway containers in my own home or hastily serving guests always seems to ruin a meal for me.

Taking a few moments to lay the table properly with a tablecloth, cutlery, napkins and candles or flowers not only adds instant charm and appeal to any dish, but it shows respect for your guests and yourself. Appropriate crockery for each element of the meal is also important and invokes a special sense of ceremony which can be sadly lacking from many modern rituals.

Candlelight softens the features of anyone's face, but also has the added effect of softening the mood. Just as conversation flows more freely when you add some good wine, special touches will make any guest at your table feel valued and relaxed. And if you're not an especially confident cook, this will get everyone in the right mood before they've even taken a bite.

# Pretty napkins and placemats

These are so simple – all you need is the right fabric and thread to begin with, and they're almost done. Tie six together with a ribbon to make a beautiful housewarming gift for a friend, or whip up a couple of sets for yourself: one for elegant evening meals and another for afternoon teas.

For smart evening dinners, I'd suggest fabric in a bold pattern and contrast – black and beige perhaps, or simple burgundy. For afternoon tea, I prefer pretty florals and have used a swatch of '50s rose-patterned linen bought for $5 in a market stall to make these. With the leftover fabric, you can cut and appliqué linen roses to another, plainer fabric to make matching placemats. Don't ask me why, but for lunch I favour simple beige or white damask, crisply ironed.

# You will need

- 1.6 m x 112 cm-wide (1³/₄ yd x 44 in) fabric
- Ruler
- Soft pencil or dressmaker's chalk
- Dressmaker's scissors
- Iron
- Sewing machine and thread

## Instructions: Napkins

1. Lay your fabric out flat and, using the ruler and dressmaker's chalk, measure and cut six 50 cm (20 in) squares. It is important to cut your squares precisely on the straight grain of the fabric, so get your fabric squared up before you start cutting.

2. Take your first square and your iron, and press under 1 cm (³/₈ in) along each raw edge.

3. Open out the edges again and you will see you have pressed a tiny 1 cm (³/₈ in) square into each corner of the napkin. Use your ruler to rule a diagonal line across each corner of the napkin at the inner corner of this little square. Trim off the corner along your ruled line. This will reduce bulk on the finished napkin and keep the corners neat.

4. Repeat for the three remaining corners of the napkin. Now press under 1 cm (³/₈ in) again on each edge as before, then press under another 1 cm (³/₈ in) on each edge and pin or tack the hems in place.

5. Stitching close to the inner pressed edge of the hem, stitch along one side of the napkin right to the edge. Leaving the needle in the fabric, lift the presser foot and swivel the fabric around so that you are sewing at right angles to the previous line of stitching. Stitch a tiny square of stitching in the corner of the napkin to hold the corner of the hem in place, pivoting on each corner, until you have completed the square and are ready to sew the next side of the hem.

6. Repeat Step 5 for each corner of the napkin.

7. Repeat Steps 2–7 for each fabric square (see, I told you they were simple!) to create a finished set of napkins. Fold and press each napkin over on itself three times before placing it to the left-hand side of the plate, under your knife and fork or on top of your smaller side plate for an elegantly laid table setting.

These are even easier to construct than the napkins, and also make great gifts for friends.

## You will need

- 0.5 m x 112 cm-wide ($^2/_3$ yd x 44 in) patterned fabric
- Same amount striped or plain cotton or linen fabric
- Ruler
- Dressmaker's chalk
- Dressmaker's scissors
- Sewing machine and thread
- Iron

## Instructions: Placemats

1. Lay your patterned fabric out flat and use the ruler and dressmaker's chalk to measure and cut six rectangles, each 22 x 32 cm (9 x 13 in).

2. Repeat Step 1 with the backing fabric.

3. With right sides together and raw edges matching, pin a fabric and backing rectangle to each other.

4. Allowing a 1 cm ($^3/_8$ in) seam, sew the rectangles together around the edges, leaving one of the shorter sides open. Trim the corners diagonally to reduce bulk.

5. Turn right side out, gently pulling out the corners with your fingers. Iron the placemat flat.

6. Press under the seam allowance on the raw edges of the opening, then use your machine to topstitch the opening closed, stitching about 3 mm ($^1/_8$ in) from the edge.

7. Topstitch the opposite end of the mat to match.

8. Repeat Steps 3–6 until you have a finished set of six placemats.

# Glowing papier mâché candle holders

I love a spot of *papier mâché* – you'll get yourself in a complete mess and probably end up scraping bits of hardened glue off your work area for days to come, but it's so much fun and will make you feel like a kid again.

These are delicate, so are probably best put together by grown-ups, but on page 138 there are instructions for making larger papier mâché sculptures which you can definitely attempt when you have little people in tow.

## You will need

- Chicken wire in a small cross-hatch (available from a hardware store or garden nursery)
- Tin snips
- Pliers
- Newspaper
- Wallpaper adhesive, mixed with water as per packet instructions
- Large bowl
- Acrylic paint and paintbrush
- Small candles or tea-lights

*Tip*

Make as many of these candle holders as you like – five or six on most tables should throw enough light to eat dinner by.

## *Instructions*

1. For each candle holder, you will need to cut a circle of chicken wire, approximately 5 cm (2 in) in diameter with your tin snips, and a rectangle 5 x 15 cm (2 x 6 in).

2. Wrap the rectangle of chicken wire around on itself from end to end to make a tube and, using pliers, bend over the edges to secure it together.

3. Place the circle of chicken wire at one end of the tube and bend the edges up to secure – this is the base of your candle holder.

4. Lay out a few sheets of newspaper on your workspace or table to protect it from drips.

5. Rip another few sheets of newspaper into 2.5–4 cm-wide (1–1$^1$/$_2$ in) strips.

6. Dip a ripped sheet into the wallpaper paste to soak, then pinch the end of the strip and run your fingers along it to remove as much of the mixture as possible.

7. Wrap the strip around your chicken-wire frame, starting at the top of the candle holder.

8. Use your strips to cover the entire frame, overlapping at the edges.

9. Turn your construction upside down and leave to dry for 24 hours, preferably in a sunny spot. (Store any unused paste in the fridge, covered with plastic.)

10. The following day, repeat Steps 6–9 to add another layer and leave to dry for another 24 hours. (You can throw away your paste or store in the fridge again, in case you've missed any bits.)

11. After 48 hours, your candle holder should be dry and ready to paint.

12. Paint white or any colour you'd like – warm tones such as red, pink or orange will throw a lovely glow over the table and be more flattering than greens or blues.

13. After your paint has dried, turn out the lights, place a small candle or tea-light inside each holder and strike a match.

# The perfect tea cosy

## You will need

- Pieces of two old wool jumpers destined for the rag bag, one large enough to fit around your teapot; the other just for a feature patch
- Wool wash
- Pinking shears
- Dressmaker's scissors
- Sewing machine and thread

## Instructions

1. Wash the wool by hand in a nicely scented wool wash and hottish water and then lay it flat on a towel to dry. The high temperature of the water will cause the wool to shrink and felt slightly, so you can cut it without fraying.

2. Wrap the larger piece of wool around your teapot, folded over at the top with the direction of the weave running downwards (which means that the stretch runs from side to side around the pot), and pin around the sides and top to work out how much fabric you will need to fit around the pot.

3. Cut out the shape of your teapot with pinking shears, adding 6 mm (1/4 in) extra all round for your seam allowance.

4. From the contrasting piece of wool, use your dressmaker's scissors to cut a decorative shape for the front of the teapot – a heart, a bird, a star, perhaps.

5. Set the sewing machine to a zigzag stitch, then sew the shape to the front of the larger piece of fabric. (I prefer to use a contrasting thread such as pink against white, or yellow against blue.)

6. Place your two tea cosy shapes together, right sides facing each other. Allowing a 6 mm (1/4 in) seam, sew around the edges of the fabric, leaving holes for the teapot's handle and spout. At the edges of the holes, reverse-stitch a few times so the seams will not come apart.

7. Turn under a hem on the bottom edge of the cosy and stitch in place.

8. Turn right side out, fill teapot with 1 teaspoon of leaves for each cup, one for the pot and freshly boiled water, then dress the pot in its new stylish outfit.

Why are most tea cosies uniformly hideous? Maybe it's because no-one uses them anymore, and they have dated terribly. Admittedly, tea bags are easier to use, but loose-leaf tea still tastes so much better – even if brewing a pot takes a little longer.

I say bring back the tea cosy! But for pity's sake, make it more attractive. The standard acrylic beanie is likely to turn people off drinking the world's best beverage altogether. And how else can we Keep Calm and Carry On?

# Eye-catching table runners

A table runner is a strip of fabric or other textile which runs down the centre length of a table, saving the surface from damage. It can also work as a decorative feature in itself for a dining, coffee, hall or dressing table, and looks far more modern than a lace doily.

Construct your table runner from one striking piece of fabric or, as I've done here, mix and match a number of pieces together for an arty patchwork.

# You will need

- Various pieces of complementary or pleasantly clashing fabrics in a range of sizes
- A strip of calico, canvas or plain fabric to back your runner
- Ruler or measuring tape
- Dressmaker's chalk
- Dressmaker's scissors or pinking shears
- Sewing machine and thread
- Iron

# Instructions

1. Most fabric nowadays is pre-shrunk, but just in case, wash, dry and press all your pieces before you start.

2. Work out how long and wide you want your runner. It's going to be centred in the middle of your table, so it will need to be wide enough to fit a serving platter, salt, pepper or other accoutrements, and can either finish before the edge of the table or hang over the sides. It's entirely up to you – mine has a finished size of 30 x 150 cm (12 x 60 in).

3. Use your ruler or measuring tape to measure out your piece of backing fabric, adding 1.5 cm (5/8 in) all round for seam allowance. Mark with chalk and cut out.

4. Lay your backing fabric on the floor or table and start to arrange your smaller pieces on it. There are no rules – use striped rectangles, floral squares, plain colours or all of these together. Just keep playing until you've covered the entire backing and you're happy with how the patterns and colours work together.

5. Start sewing your patchwork pieces together. Because they're all in different sizes, I get too confused about where they're meant to go if I take them to the machine all at once. Sew them together, two at a time, thinking ahead about the overlapping seams and how you can avoid unpicking them at the edges to include another piece. You should also iron the seams as you go – some will need to be pressed open and some can be pressed to one side. Do whatever is going to be least bulky.

6. When you've sewn all your patchwork pieces together, turn your completed piece of fabric over and iron it as flat as possible again.

7. Snip away any loose threads or excess fabric, being careful not to cut into your stitching.

8. Line up the patchwork strip with your backing, right sides together.

9. Stitch around the edges, allowing a 1.5 cm (5/8 in) seam and leaving one of the shorter sides open. Trim the corners diagonally to reduce bulk.

10. Turn runner right side out, pushing out the corners carefully and press well.

11. Press under the seam allowance on each raw edge of the opening, then use your machine to topstitch it closed, stitching about 6 mm (1/4 in) from the edge and continuing the topstitching around all edges, if you like.

12. Press the whole thing thoroughly again. Now admire your gorgeous work.

*Sitting rooms to swoon over*

# Cosy cushions and upholstery

Apart from the kitchen, the sitting or living room is the one place in the home that you're likely to spend the most time awake. If it's not inspiring, relaxing and comfortable, you need to fix this sooner rather than later.

Neutrals are a great base for any room, but so very bland on the eye when filling a space from floor to ceiling. The easiest way to liven up staid furniture in muted colours is with colourful, quirky cushions, throws, lampshades and *objets d'art*, such as vases, ceramics or knick-knacks, collected on your travels. None of these need be a huge investment, although coordinating a knockout big-ticket item such as a designer rug with something collected from a skip and spruced up a bit can create a magical combination. Stylists work with similar contrasts of high and low all the time, to great effect. Such contrasts create visual interest and character in any space.

The Japanese have perfected the art of the placement of objects and I take their lead, moving things around often to see what works. In our living space, I have lots of gorgeous coffee table books on display, on subjects from fashion to gardening and history to cooking. I change them often so I don't 'stop seeing' them, and also rotate a small selection of favourite items to keep the room from looking stale. This can be anything from an interesting branch collected from the nature strip after a heavy wind, or pebbles from a Barcelona beach arrayed on my mantelpiece, to pretty cards, beaten-up candlesticks and garish pottery from the '60s. A necessary fixture, apart from books, is my husband's guitar. Both ensure we can relax and while away the hours even when the TV is off. Style your living space like this to reflect shifting moods, and it will always engage you.

For the larger items, don't forget that a boring piece of furniture can easily be updated with new upholstery or a lick of paint. My most

treasured piece of furniture is a '20s club lounge, bought for a paltry sum at an auction house, where it had been languishing for months. The previous owner bought it from a wealthy socialite 20 years earlier, but had let his bulldog live on it for the past few years, slashing its royal blue fabric to shreds with his paws. I had the fabric and foam padding replaced, and the intricately carved wooden panels at the head and feet French-polished. I love that this grand old item has been given a new lease of life. I didn't dare reupholster it myself, so it wasn't exactly cheap, but it's a piece I know I'll always have in my home. In its new guise, it should easily survive for another 80 years or more.

# Floor cushions to sink into

The various share-houses I lived in throughout university had an abundance of floor cushions in lieu of furniture. We took turns sitting on the one sofa someone's parents had generously donated, while the rest of us lounged on cushions, watching films or chatting.

Floor cushions aren't just for poor students. In flats and smaller houses, they can be arranged around the coffee table to provide a cosy alternative eating area when you find yourself with more guests than chairs. They're also great for parties and video days when you have lots of friends over.

# *You will need*

- 73 cm (29 in) square for the cushion top (a single piece, or make up a square of patchwork fabric)
- 73 x 76 cm (29 x 30$^1$/$_4$ in) fabric, for the backing (if you have a light or thin fabric for the top that's fine, but you'll want to use something sturdier and darker on the floor side, like indigo denim)
- 65 cm (25 in) zipper
- 70 cm (28 in) square cushion insert
- Ruler
- Dressmaker's chalk
- Dressmaker's scissors or pinking shears
- Sewing machine and thread

# *Instructions*

1. Measure and cut your backing rectangle into two pieces: one should be 73 x 14.5 cm (29 x 5$^3$/$_4$ in) and the other should be 73 x 61.5 cm (29 x 24$^1$/$_2$ in).

2. With right sides together, align the two backing pieces along the 73 cm (29 in) edge.

3. Lay the zip along this 73 cm (29 in) edge so that it is equidistant from both ends. Make a mark on the edges of the fabric to show where the zip opening should start and finish.

4. Put the zip aside and, allowing a 1.5 cm ($^5$/$_8$ in) seam, sew the seam closed at each end, from your mark to the edge, leaving the seam open in the middle. Press the seam allowance open, pressing open the edges of the unstitched section as well.

5. With the right side of the fabric facing upwards, position your closed zip under the opening (make sure it's facing up the right way) and pin it in place. Pin one folded edge of the opening about 2 mm ($^1$/$_{16}$ in) from the zipper teeth and the pin the other side about 1 cm ($^3$/$_8$ in) from the folded edge. Place a pin across the seam at the top and bottom of the opening, one pin just above the pull tab and the other just below the zip stop. Tack the zip in position before stitching it, as the pins can get a bit awkward while you stitch.

6. Using a zipper foot on your machine, sew the zip in place, stitching along both sides and pivoting on the needle at the corners to stitch across the top and bottom too. You should now have a cushion back that measures 73 cm (29 in) square.

7. Open the zip about 2.5 cm (1 in). With right sides together, raw edges matching and allowing a 1.5 cm ($^5$/$_8$ in) seam, stitch the cushion front to the back around all edges.

8. Snip diagonally across each corner to remove the extra fabric – take care not to cut into your stitching – and turn the cover right side out through the zip opening. Push the corners out with your fingers.

9. Insert the cushion pad into your cover and zip it up. Done!

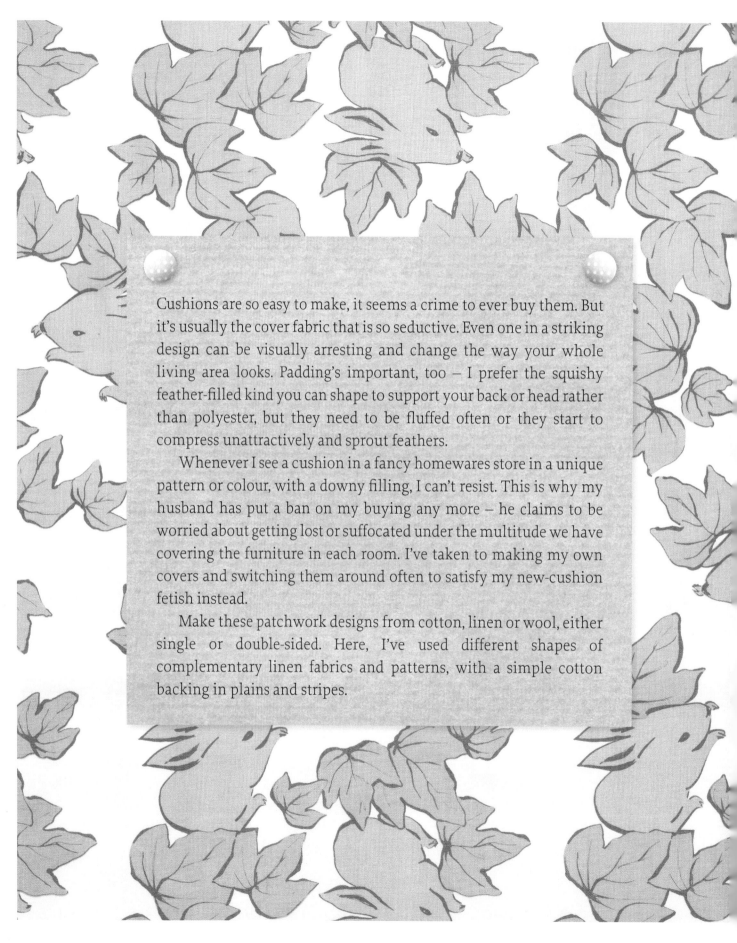

Cushions are so easy to make, it seems a crime to ever buy them. But it's usually the cover fabric that is so seductive. Even one in a striking design can be visually arresting and change the way your whole living area looks. Padding's important, too – I prefer the squishy feather-filled kind you can shape to support your back or head rather than polyester, but they need to be fluffed often or they start to compress unattractively and sprout feathers.

Whenever I see a cushion in a fancy homewares store in a unique pattern or colour, with a downy filling, I can't resist. This is why my husband has put a ban on my buying any more – he claims to be worried about getting lost or suffocated under the multitude we have covering the furniture in each room. I've taken to making my own covers and switching them around often to satisfy my new-cushion fetish instead.

Make these patchwork designs from cotton, linen or wool, either single or double-sided. Here, I've used different shapes of complementary linen fabrics and patterns, with a simple cotton backing in plains and stripes.

# Sumptuously soft patchwork cushions

## You will need

- Various pieces of fabric, either in squares or mismatched shapes, to make a piece of patchwork fabric 53 cm (21 in) square (remember to allow 1.5 cm ($^5/8$ in) seam allowance around each piece)
- 53 x 74 cm (21 x 29 in) piece plain fabric in cotton, denim or canvas, for backing
- Ruler
- Dressmaker's chalk
- Dressmaker's scissors or pinking shears
- Sewing machine and thread
- Iron
- 50 cm (20 in) square cushion insert
- Large press studs (optional)

## *Instructions*

1. Measure and cut your backing rectangle into two pieces: one should be 53 x 30 cm (21 x 12 in) and the other should be 53 x 44 cm (21 x 17 in).

2. Press under 1.5 cm ($^5/_8$ in) on one 53 cm (21 in) edge of each backing piece, then press under another 1.5 cm ($^5/_8$ in) on the same edge and stitch the hem in place on each piece along the inner edge.

3. Lay your backing pieces on the table with right sides facing up and hemmed edges adjacent to each other. Now lap the hemmed edge of the shorter piece over the hemmed edge of the longer piece until the sides measure 53 cm (21 in). Machine-baste the lapped edges along the sides to hold them in place.

4. You should now have a cushion back that measures 53 cm (21 in) square.

5. Lay down the cushion back and arrange your patchwork over it, swapping the pieces around for the prettiest combination.

6. Sew your patchwork pieces together to create a finished size of 53 x 53 cm (21 x 21 in). Keep your iron handy and press each piece as you add it, pressing the seams open or to one side, whichever seems less bulky.

7. When you've finished, iron the patchwork thoroughly so the seams lie flat, and snip off any loose threads or excess fabric.

8. With right sides together, raw edges matching and allowing a 1.5 cm ($^5/_8$ in) seam, stitch the patchwork cushion front to the back around all edges.

9. Snip diagonally across each corner to remove the extra fabric – take care not to cut into your stitching – and turn the cover right side out through the lapped opening. Push the corners out with your fingers.

10. Insert the cushion pad into your cover. If you want to, you can add 2–3 press studs to the lapped opening to keep it closed, but this shouldn't be necessary – the lapped section should keep the cushion insert neatly concealed.

11. Throw cushion on the sofa and start using immediately.

# Braided rug

## You will need

- Three strips of fabric, about 8 m (8³/₄ yd) in length by 10 cm (4 in) wide for a finished rug of approximately 1 m (39 in) in diameter. You don't need 8 m (8³/₄ yd) of fabric, though – cut strips from an old sheet or clothes and stitch the ends together to create the length
- Dressmaker's scissors
- Sewing needle and thread
- Large safety pin
- Strong elastic band or hair band
- Optional covered button for the centre

## Instructions

1. When you've constructed your three 8 m (8³/₄ yd) long strips of fabric, hold all three ends together in a T-shape, then stitch a line in the centre where the pieces meet.

2. Use your safety pin to pin the hair band (hair bands are less likely to snap than elastic bands) to the joined end of the fabric strips. Loop the band around a door handle.

3. Start plaiting your three strips together, just as you would braid someone's hair, and move away from the door handle as the plait grows longer to keep the line taut and the tension the same throughout the braid.

4. Tuck the cut or frayed edges under as you plait the fabric together. This will make the top surface of the rug smoother. Don't worry about the places where the fabric strips are joined: just roll the raw edges under.

5. When you've finished, unloop the band from the door handle and use the safety pin to secure the unstitched end, then stitch across the ends to secure them as before.

6. Take one end and place it on the floor or a table, then wind the braid around the centre, smoother side facing upwards.

7. Use your needle and thread to sew the braid together, winding it around as you go, from the inside out. Keep the braid lying on a flat surface and sew around it without pulling it, so it will sit just as flat when it's finished. Large stitches are fine, and you can either hide or make a feature of them with thread in a contrasting colour.

8. Snip off any loose threads or frayed edges.

9. Sew your covered button to the centre if you fancy the look – it shouldn't interfere with your or your animal friend's comfort when sitting or walking over it.

Braided rugs have a homespun charm that is very appealing, but they don't always need to look like something out of the American Midwest. Avoid chintz and go for fabric in monochromes or even one colour, such as beige. You'll find the finished look is surprisingly elegant, and will make a very stylish rug for an end table or even for your pet to lie on by the fire.

Here, I've cut strips from fabric in three different colours, and plaited them together to create a simple design. When I had enough for a good-sized circle, I switched the red fabric with cream cotton to give the rug a border.

# Ribbon lampshade

Lampshade bases in good working order are easy to find in thrift stores and local markets but often have damaged, ugly or missing shades. IKEA and other homewares stores often have a good range of simple bases if you can't find one you like. You might even consider having a favourite vase turned into a lamp by an electrician – chinois and garish '60s vases in turquoise or orange look magic when given this treatment.

It's quite simple to make your own shade to match, using wallpaper or fabric, but a bit fiddly. The easiest solution is to wrap ribbon around your frame, secured by a few stitches. I find that a plain shade with a decorative base often works best, or vice versa. This ribbon lampshade is inspired by a beautiful shade the talented interior designer Rebecca Furzer made me, but I've substituted her clever raw silk strips with ribbons to simplify the construction.

## You will need

- Cylindrical wire lampshade frame – mine is 33 cm (13 in) in diameter and 30 cm (12 in) high
- Ribbon (velvet or grosgrain are my favourites, but you can use any kind you like. The length will depend on the size of your frame and how densely you want to weave your ribbon. Here, I've used about 15 m (16½ yd) of ribbon in total, in two shades (7.5 m x 20 mm-wide (8¼ yd x ⅞ in) in one shade, and 7.5 m x 25 mm-wide (8¼ yd x 1 in) in another)
- Dressmaker's scissors
- Needle and thread

## Instructions

1. Fold the end of your ribbon over the bottom edge of your frame and stitch into place with needle and thread, making sure the end of the ribbon is facing inwards.

2. Pull your length of ribbon up, keeping it taut; take it over the top edge and back down again, then back under the bottom edge. Continue weaving it around from the top to bottom edge until you get back to the beginning.

3. Stitch the end into place, with the end of the ribbon again facing inwards.

4. If you want to use a contrasting ribbon, repeat this process, weaving in and out of the spaces between your first ribbon.

*Get arty*

## Forget the town – paint your home red (and cobalt, magenta and lemon) to suit your mood

When I was in my teens, I had a friend whose father was a sculptor. I used to adore visiting his home – a small three-bedroom cottage and garden where the family had lived for almost two decades. The love, happiness and shared history in that house were virtually palpable and very infectious. Coming from a family of gypsies who moved almost once a year to increasingly modern abodes, to me their home seemed a magical place. It housed the artistic efforts of all four family members and boasted a stunning variety of creative pursuits, often inspired by their beloved sausage dog, Buddha: from driftwood and chicken-wire sculptures living in the garden, to paintings, *papier mâché*, mosaic tiling, ceramics, patchwork quilts and more.

I would marvel at the living room walls, literally covered from skirting board to cornice with items that held some meaning to them – all homemade or given by other artists. An hour sitting in their lovely hand-covered armchairs was not enough to take it all in. The overall effect was warm, inviting and thoroughly inspiring. Back then, I vowed to one day own my own home and fill it with such precious objects.

It makes me sad to think that, over the years of shifting around, we divested ourselves of virtually all meaningful items. My friend's house conveyed more about the lives of the people who occupied it than even a lengthy novel could. I don't think I've ever felt so convinced of a family or person's essence – what makes them uniquely 'them' – in a house since.

# Clever collages and paintings

There is a school of thought – particularly followed by artists themselves – that bare walls are better than those embellished with prints rather than originals. I don't necessarily subscribe to this (somewhat snobbish) view but I can see the point: as paintings are now mass-reproduced in high quality laser prints, anyone can afford to own a Klimt or a Warhol. But why not go for originals if you can, to make your home unique and unlike everyone else's? And you can: by making them yourself.

When I moved into my home, I had so many bare white walls to fill but not the budget to buy the kind of art I liked, so I started painting and making collages of my own. The first was very simple – a dot painting made from a white-painted canvas decorated with shades of pink, yellow and orange. I applied the dots by dipping cotton buds into acrylic paint and then directly onto the canvas. The effect was fun and fresh, a riot of colour complementing the other shades in the room. It didn't matter that I had no skills as an artist. I thought I'd get rid of it in time but it's still hanging in a bedroom and I'm considering having it fitted with a thin beechwood frame.

185

## 𝒴ou will need

- ⊙ Canvases or cardboard (from arts supplies shops or, as mine are, from discount stores which I still refer to as 'two-dollar shops' but which don't supply much of anything anymore in this price bracket)
- ⊙ A selection of acrylic paints in black, white and primary colours
- ⊙ Glue stick or spray adhesive
- ⊙ Paper scissors
- ⊙ Cut-up cards, fabric and magazines
- ⊙ Any other ribbons, buttons, stickers or shiny things that take your fancy
- ⊙ Spray-on laminate (optional)

Collages are also easy if you don't have any drawing skills. I can't bear to throw away wedding invitations or pretty cards given by friends. Instead I hoard them in boxes and go through them every few years. It's a pleasant way to spend a few hours. The last time I did this, I had the idea to display some of the most striking and special in a collage.

I've always loved classic silhouettes and cameo brooches, so I drew a silhouette of a lady in a Victorian dress in pencil. I then filled in her head and hands with black paint and started to glue my favourite cut-up images onto the dress area. This is a fun way to play with colours and styling – here, I've used a magazine cutting of Daphne du Maurier (author of the terrific gothic romance, *Rebecca*) alongside pictures of flower sprays, wisps of lace and wedding invitations. I then used a glossy cream paint to lacquer the surface of the dress and wash out the images a little.

In her outstretched hand, my lady is holding a card shaped like an old travel trunk's label, with the words *Bon Voyage* on it. Our friends Patti and Scott gave us this card a month after our wedding, as my husband and I were packing up our things to move overseas. Every time I look at her, the anonymous bride is a visual reminder of all the wonderful weddings we attended that year, and our beloved friends on the other side of the world.

Animals are also easy to draw and paint – they really don't need to be perfect, and can even be just be a suggestion of shape, as with the white bulldog here. They really brighten a child's room, and make a whimsical addition to any other area of the house. My bulldog is painted on a very small, almost postcard-sized canvas and the baby giraffe on a slightly larger one. Both hang just above my pantry door. The giraffe is thinking 'I don't know why' in French because a) I think everything sounds better in French and b) he's such an odd-looking creature, I imagine him to be as perplexed by evolution as I am.

When I was seven months pregnant, I started decorating our spare room (once my walk-in wardrobe, sob sob) for the arrival of our daughter. At first I thought a framed vintage candy poster from the '50s would look great and be bright and pretty, but couldn't find one that was just right on the many websites I spent hours trawling.

Instead, I bought two pieces of cardboard and some masking tape to tape them together, and drew an outline of an elephant. I painted the exterior a dark grey and the interior silver, and a big blue eye fringed with long lashes. I then cut around the outline. The rest is a collage of remnant deckchair fabric for the saddle, rickrack, ribbons and wrapping paper, and a silk fake flower salvaged from a charity shop. It took me no longer than an hour to make and is much more original than the reproduction poster I had in mind.

If you don't feel confident drawing freeform, try tracing a picture or shape you like and then blowing it up on a photocopier before cutting it out and tracing it onto your cardboard or canvas.

# Fabric canvases

## You will need

- Wooden stretcher frame (from any art supplies shop. The best are made from good quality wood, with tongue and groove corners that fit into each other with a little help from a hammer tap.)
- Fabric to fit the frame (enough to cover the surface, sides and an extra few centimetres to tuck neatly out of sight against the wall)
- Iron
- Staple gun and staples

Sometimes I'm blown away by the sheer creativity that must be involved in coming up with new prints and patterns and making colour palettes work on cloth. Fabric design goes so far beyond the utilitarian – paired with necessary wearability, good fabric design seems to me to be nothing short of genius.

Fabric designers are artisans, capturing the mood of the times just as poignantly as clothes designers, writers, musicians, filmmakers, painters and sculptors do, with their aesthetics distilling and portraying the essence of entire generations. Think of those stunning patterns from William Morris, Laura Ashley, Marimekko, Celia Birtwell and Florence Broadhurst.

If you find a fabric or print that speaks to you, frame it the way you would a unique piece of art. Just the act of taking it out of its everyday context will render it unique in itself.

## Instructions

1. Iron your fabric flat on the wrong side.

2. Centre your frame on the wrong side of the fabric, then fold up the edges of one side and staple along the edge at 5–8 cm (2–3 in) intervals.

3. When you get to a corner, fold the fabric carefully around the edge as though you were wrapping a gift, then staple in place.

4. Continue until you've finished all four sides, and your piece will be ready to hang.

# Lino printing

I took a course in printmaking recently, planning to learn how to screen print my own patterns onto cloth. The course description was a bit vague and I didn't give it too much thought after signing up, so my friend Lisa and I found ourselves stumbling into nine weeks of instruction on etching and dry-point. What a happy discovery – we had so much fun learning this delicate art, although using the elaborate presses needed to make our prints meant we couldn't continue working once we'd left the studio.

I was keen to keep using what I had learnt and discovered lino printing – a simple and inexpensive way to make your own striking prints at home.

Use your lino prints to make greeting cards or framed gifts for friends. You don't need to be talented at drawing – the effect is so unique, you'll find even abstract lines and geometric patterns will look fantastic when inked and printed.

## *You will need*

- Sheets of lino (from an art supplies store)
- A lino cutter
- Pencil or ball-point pen
- Lino carving tools – usually sold in a set of 6 with steel blades in different sizes to create a variety of effects
- Block printing ink
- Roller
- Paper or parchment
- Watercolours or acrylic paints

## *Instructions*

1. Cut your lino to the size you want, perhaps starting with a small square.

2. Use your pencil or ball-point pen to sketch an image onto the surface of the lino.

3. Experiment with the carving tools to cut away the areas inside your outline, creating a stencil. Thick outlines work best with this form of printing. Remember that you're going to end up with a mirror image of what you've cut out, so letters or numerals won't work unless you trace them in reverse onto your lino.

4. Dip the roller into your ink, making sure the ink is spread evenly, then roll over the surface of the lino stencil.

5. Lay your paper face down on your stencil, then rub along the back of the paper to transfer the ink to the paper.

6. Use watercolours or acrylic paint to fill in the white spaces if you want to add some colour to your print.

## *Grandma never looked so good*

# Modern patchwork quilts and throws

In the postwar era, the Western world experienced a huge leap in individual wealth. People still had the skills to mend and re-fashion tired or broken things in their homes, but with the abundance of new appliances and products available on the market, they increasingly found that they didn't need or want to. Consequently, the art of patchworking declined in popularity and was practised on a much smaller scale than previously.

Patchwork is simply cutting up old or damaged fabric and reworking it to make something new, such as a cushion cover, curtains or a throw. This is a wonderful way to give fabrics a second lease of life, but the tradition has not always been about thrift.

Once it was considered very special to give a patchwork quilt as a wedding gift. Often created by a group of women, made up of both friends and family working together, they would gather new and old pieces, using elements such as a favourite childhood dress or piece of clothing worn by the bride or groom, and even fabric salvaged from their own parents' wedding quilt to fashion into a beautiful new item. In this way, history provided a context for the happy couple's new life. It was a way to wish them love, happiness and many children together, and the gift would be destined to spend the rest of its life on the marriage bed.

The Whitney Otto book *How to Make an American Quilt* (also made into a film starring Winona Ryder and the fabulous Anne Bancroft) is

based on this tradition, the quilt of the title acting as a catalyst for the retelling of the main characters' romances. As with any revival of the old, there is a story to be told, a rich layering of history that informs the present. The art of patchworking is not dead, as evidenced by the recent revival of quilting in particular.

By now you will know not to throw out anything without thinking of its potential for crafty projects, but start thinking of the items closer to home: those garments or household linen languishing in your wardrobe or linen cupboard that you haven't used in the last two years. Old sheets, knits and summer shirts or dresses all make brilliant sources for a patchwork quilt or throw. Consider putting away for later those really special pieces, such as a child's favourite outfit that they've since grown out of, a cocktail dress you wore on many fun evenings, or an angora knit which was worn to death before you shrunk it by accident in the wash. And keep your eye out for new or second-hand fabrics to complement them.

By making your own patchwork, especially from secondhand and pre-loved fabrics, you are contributing to a rich and colourful tradition of reinvention and giving depth to your own creativity. It should give you a thrill to realise that the special memories attached to your old clothes can still be a part of your life, even when the garments cease to be useful in their original form.

As much as I admire the quilts other people make, I haven't the patience myself for cutting out all those squares and tricky shapes, or for fiddling around with perfect padding. This is the easy version, to be thrown over a duvet for a simpler, but still simply gorgeous, finish. Construct the front of the quilt, sew it to a flat sheet backing and fill with a feathery duvet – it makes a very special wedding gift.

'Just Married'
patchwork duvet cover

## *You will need*

- One queen-sized flat sheet (Egyptian cotton in the highest thread-count you can afford is ideal, but an old sheet, softened by many washes, works just as well. Alternatively, you might also want to use a sheet in flannelette, or buy sheeting by the metre.)
- Pretty patches of fabric, to make a finished size to match your flat sheet (I used 9 different fabrics, plus a 10th fabric for a centre motif)
- Feather duvet in duck or goose down (see Tip, opposite)
- Iron
- Sewing machine and thread

## *Instructions*

1. Lay your sheet on the floor and arrange your patchwork pieces over it until you've covered the entire sheet and you're happy with how the patterns and colours work together. I used a 32 cm (12³/₄ in) square (30 cm (12 in) finished size) as my basic building block, basing the patchwork on a size of 7 squares across x 7 squares down, which is a perfect queen-sized cover (210 cm (84 in) square when finished). However, because I wanted to incorporate my beautiful central motif – which was about 47 x 51 cm (18¹/₂ x 20 in) – I added rectangles and strips to this centre piece, till it was equal to a three x three square block – making everything very easy to sew together. Do whatever works for you. My only other tip is to make sure that your squares and rectangles are cut on the straight grain of the fabric – if you cut pieces on the bias (diagonal) grain, the edges will stretch and your cover will not lie flat.

2. To reduce the possibility of fraying, zigzag around all the edges of each patchwork piece – this might seem tedious, but it really is important, as your cover is going to be washed fairly frequently.

3. Lay out all your pieces on the floor or bed in the right order. Allowing a 1 cm (³/₈ in) seam, sew the patchwork pieces together, one after another. If you have a centre motif, sew the border pieces to that first, then sew your squares into rows and finally, sew all the rows together to complete the top.

4. Use your iron to press each piece as you sew, pressing the seam allowance to the same side in each row and varying the side to which you press in every alternate row – this will make everything less bulky when the rows are stitched together.

5. When you've sewn all your patchwork pieces together, press the completed top carefully so that it is as flat as possible and snip away any loose threads.

6. Line up the patchwork fabric with your backing sheet, right sides together, and trim the edges, if necessary, so both pieces are the same size. Try to position the finished turn-back edge of your sheet at the bottom opening edge of the cover.

7. Now, with wrong sides together and allowing a 6 mm ($^1/_4$ in) seam, stitch the front and back of the cover together around the edges, starting and finishing one square in on the bottom opening edge.

8. Clip diagonally across the seam allowance on the corners and turn the cover inside out, so the right sides are together.

9. Now stitch the seam again, this time allowing a 1 cm ($^3/_8$ in) seam. (This double seam is called a French seam – it is very strong and prevents fraying.)

10. Turn the cover right side out through the bottom opening.

11. Press under 6 mm ($^1/_4$ in), then another 1 cm ($^3/_8$ in) along the raw opening edge of the patchwork and stitch the hem in place near the inner edge. (If you haven't been able to use the finished edge of your sheet, you will need to turn under and stitch a hem on this edge as well.)

12. From leftover scraps of your patchwork fabric, cut eight 3 x 33 cm ($1^1/_4$ x 13 in) strips, for the ties.

13. Using your iron, press under 6 mm ($^1/_4$ in) on all edges of each tie. Now press the ties in half lengthwise, wrong sides together. Topstitch close to all edges.

14. Starting at the third square in along the bottom opening edge, stitch four ties to the opening, positioning them at each patchwork seam, or at even intervals. Stitch the remaining ties to the sheet edge, to match.

15. Insert your duvet and tie neat bows.

*Tip*

Pillows, duvets and cushion inserts are among the few things I will never buy second-hand. Clothes can be washed if you don't know where they've been, but second-hand bedding will harbour dust mites and other nasties you don't want to be breathing in at close quarters.

# Woolly patchwork throws

## You will need

- A selection of old jumpers in pure wools and complementary colours – how many will depend on their size, but 4 large men's ones or 5 – 6 smaller women's jumpers should be more than enough. Round- or polo-necked jumpers will have more available fabric than V-necks. Go for tighter knits if you can: big loopy lace styles might unravel if you're too scared to shrink them a lot, and don't be afraid to experiment with colour. My jumpers are sourced from charity shops. They don't all need to be made out of the same wool – patches of fluffy angora or mohair can work really well contrasted against flatter merino or lambswool styles
- About 7 m x 5 cm-wide (7²/₃ yd x 2 in) bias binding in a matching or contrasting colour – this is more than enough for a 120 x 170 cm (47 x 66 in) throw
- A gentle, delicious-smelling wool wash or soap flakes (from a supermarket)
- Ruler
- Pencil
- Tracing paper or cardboard
- Paper scissors
- Dressmaker's scissors or pinking shears
- Bobble-headed pins
- Sewing machine and thread

People have very different ideas about how you should behave on your sofa. I use mine like a day bed, strewn as it is with lots of cushions and rugs for comfort, particularly in autumn and winter. I impose no rules about feet on the sofa (as long as they're bare and clean), and it's here I drink copious cups of tea, spend hours engrossed in books and magazines, write, watch telly, doze, sew and chat on the phone. It's my very own 'mission control': a home office and relaxation centre rolled into one. For me, throws are almost as essential as cushions in creating this environment. There's nothing nicer than curling up with a hot drink or glass of wine, tucking your toes under a throw for warmth or pulling one, shawl-like, across your shoulders.

When I first met my husband, he took me away for the weekend to his parents' farmhouse in Somerset, England. It was my first meeting with his parents and I was, understandably, nervous, but the Dousts were so warm and made me feel so welcome in their home, that I relaxed almost immediately. Waking up early on Sunday morning, I made myself a cup of tea, grabbed a big hardcover book on gardening and curled up on the sofa. I had no inhibitions about drawing my bare feet up to stretch out and tucked my toes under the throw at one end. This is how his mother found me, half an hour later – I think I may have been taking one too many liberties (especially at such an early stage), but she behaved graciously and has always treated her Australian daughter-in-law like one of the family, despite my casual antipodean behaviour.

This throw is so easy – you'll spend more time collecting, washing, cutting up and laying out the fabric than you will actually putting it together. I'm not a speedy sewer and the first time I attempted one, I had it finished in less than a few hours.

# *Instructions*

1. Wash your jumpers either by hand in warm (not hot!) water or, if you have a gentle wool wash setting, in your washing machine. Don't use any harsh detergents. Soap flakes or a scented wool wash will soften up the knits, even while they're slightly shrinking. When finished, lay them out flat to dry; pulling them into shape if you need to.

2. Use your ruler and pencil to rule up a 25 cm (10 in) square on tracing paper or cardboard and cut out with your paper scissors. This will be your pattern.

3. Lay the first jumper out flat and pin the pattern to the bottom hem (basque), nearest to the left-hand seam.

4. Cut out your square, then unpin the pattern. Put the square aside, making sure the right side is facing up.

5. Move your pattern across the jumper and repeat Steps 3 and 4 until you have used all available 25 x 25 cm (10 x 10 in) sections of the jumper. This should give you approximately eight squares from the front and back sections and, if you cut off the sleeves and open them up along the sleeve seam, another two – giving you 10 squares in all from one men's jumper. You will need 35 squares in total.

6. Lay out your squares, five across by seven down, to see how they work together and what appeals to you. I like a random layout, but you can alternate colours so the effect is more uniform – whichever takes your fancy.

7. Carefully stack them back together, right sides still facing upwards, so they are in the order you want them to be sewn together. I tend to go from left to right, and lay them in separate piles just to make sure I don't get them mixed up.

8. Start sewing them together on your machine, allowing a 6 mm ($^1/_4$ in) seam. I suggest sewing the horizontal rows of five first. This will be easier, as you are sewing only the sides of the squares together. Then start sewing the rows together, one after another, making sure you line up the squares from top to bottom. This will require a little more care when you get to the seams where four squares intersect.

9. Using your iron, press your bias binding in half along the length, wrong sides together. Slip the folded binding over the edge of your throw and pin it in place around the edges. Make sure you allow enough binding at each corner to allow for turning the corner, folding under the excess neatly at the corner (see Tip, below). Sew the binding in place as pinned. Your throw is finished – don't worry about the unfinished edges at the back. They won't unravel because the knits have been pre-shrunk.

10. Use the throw on your sofa, and feel free to play with the square sizes for larger or smaller throws, say, for your bed, or a child's.

# *Tip*

 It can be quite tricky to take bias binding neatly around 90-degree corners. It's much simpler to trim each corner into a gentle curve (trace round a dinner plate as a guide) and you'll find that attaching the binding is a cinch!

*Relish the opportunity to hunker down and get cosy*

# winter

My good friend Maggie once reminded me – because I knew, but had somehow forgotten – that winter might be a time of cold comfort, but it's also an important stage in the life cycle. The trees are bare and wind whips along the streets, chapping our lips and frizzing our hair, but there's so much teeming beneath the surface and getting ready to burst into bloom once the long-awaited days of spring arrive. Like the weather outside, we can start to feel cheerless and unchanging, but there's much to be celebrated about this season, just like any other. Along with the garden, we are going through a transformation, even if it's not apparent to the people around us or even ourselves.

Although I love the warm weather and particularly adore the temperate climate of autumn and spring, winter is the perfect time to hunker down and regroup, on your own and with those you love most. What better excuse for a day inside watching classic old films, or slow-cooking hearty casseroles with generous slugs of red wine? Or for a spot of list-making. It's a great time to think about where you are in life and where you want to be, and I try to take advantage of the increased time indoors by planning ahead for career, home, family and friends. Rather than my customary despair when the weather turns ugly, I've learned to love miserable days. And as the silver-lining people say when it rains, *it's good for the farmers.*

# Some suggestions to keep your spirits up during the long winter months

◎ Start an ambitious project, stitching a patchwork quilt or knitting a jumper, and spend the darkest afternoons in front of the fire, working on it.

◎ Clad your feet in sheepskin. Ugg boots might not be the most stylish fashion statement, but I challenge you to give them up once you've wiggled your toes in their gorgeous warmth and softness – they are the ultimate in comfort. And you can always reserve them for the house (although I don't).

◎ Drink lots of water and hot, caffeine-free herbal teas or honey and lemon. When the weather becomes cooler it's easy to forget to drink enough, but indoor heating is often more dehydrating than the warmer air, so it's important to keep your fluids up to stave off colds and tiredness.

◎ Burn delicious candles and oils; citrus oils, such as orange blossom or grapefruit (I love the French word for grapefruit, *pamplemousse*) are particularly zingy and will give your home a lift, and good quality soy wax candles are the ultimate in self-pampering.

◎ Don't forget to open the windows once in a while to let in some fresh air.

◎ Go for bracing walks and keep up your exercise – it's the easiest way to boost your energy levels and will stop you emerging at the end of the winter months as pale and bloated as a grub.

◎ Throw lots of fabulous candlelit dinner parties and small soirées for your closest friends and family. If your home is warm and inviting and you love being in it, it will give you a thrill to share it with others. You don't need to be a fabulous cook: soups and casseroles are easy-peasy to make but will warm anyone's heart and have people hankering to visit you again.

# Take to your bed

There was a time when I thought nothing of hobbling myself in the name of fashion. I had a wardrobe full of beautiful, vertiginous shoes – my 'killer heels' (so called because wearing them was like experiencing a slow and painful death from the ankles down). Never mind that they changed my walk from a slope-shouldered lope to a rangy, kittenish swing; a podiatrist would have a field day correcting the effects of all those years wearing the footwear equivalent of an iron maiden. Back then, I was also sleeping on a futon. And this last point, more than anything, should be an indication as to how much my priorities have changed over the years.

Nowadays, I'm all about comfort, pure and simple. This pertains to everything from footwear to bedding. Fashion mavens tend to consider this incredibly lazy, but try judging any new item of clothing by the level of comfort you feel wearing it and you'll start to notice the difference. Life suddenly becomes a bit more relaxed. Possibly a bit less glamorous, but certainly more relaxed.

The change in my life became complete when I fell pregnant and gave birth. Having a baby somehow makes you feel like babying yourself. I think it has a lot to do with the effect childbearing has on your poor body. Hobbling about both before and after, I became conscious of every itchy, uncomfortable thing touching my skin, and wanted it off more than Macbeth did the blood on his hands. Out went mohair, waist-cinching belts, 15-centimetre (6-inch) heels half a size too small and my spray-on skinny jeans. In came sheepskin, soft cotton and swaddling myself in layers of cashmere all year round. After decades spent draping myself in statement clothes covered in complicated beading and details you need a PhD to undo, I finally 'got' basics: the white cotton tee; the black cardigan, the stretch jersey dress that falls perfectly. Not only are

they chic and easy to coordinate, but the foundation of the basic wardrobe staple is comfort. It's to make you feel more like you're wearing your clothes, and less like they're wearing you.

Similarly, bed linen is another area where comfort is key. Don't believe it when you hear that thread count doesn't make a difference. Go for Egyptian cotton sheets in as high a count you can afford. Top them off with a feather duvet so fluffy the RSPCA will want to put you on their hit list. And note how much more time you enjoy spending in bed. Hell, why not block out an entire day in your diary to do just that, curling up with the papers or a new novel? Put the phone on silent. Call in sick.

Style is important – essential if you want to look good – but comfort is the secret to feeling better in your own skin. And it's a happy day indeed when you can marry both. So here are some ideas for spoiling yourself without sacrificing either.

# Warm-all-night hot water bottle cover

I hadn't seen a hot water bottle since I was a child in my grandmother's house and was sent to bed with one on a cold night, until I was browsing in a chic little boutique recently. It was covered in the softest, most stylish pale grey lambswool but the price tag made me gasp. When I next had a stomach ache I thought of it, and had this idea for my own version.

An embarrassingly simple variation on the traditional hand-knitted hot water bottle cover, I've simply found some old (somewhat holey) cashmere sweaters in my local charity store, hand washed the horrible mothball smell out of them with a eucalyptus-scented wool wash, then cut and sewn them together, avoiding the holes. I've appliquéd a heart motif to the front for decoration, but another option is to embroider words or a name to the front if it's a gift. How about simply *chaud*? It's French for hot!

## You will need

- A hot water bottle (from a chemist or supermarket)
- A wool jumper, freshly laundered (a tighter knit is best, as the sewn edges of chunkier styles might not hold up in the wash)
- Another small piece of felt or tightly knitted wool in a contrasting colour or pattern
- Tracing paper and pencil
- Paper scissors
- Dressmaker's scissors
- Pins
- Needle and thread, or a sewing machine

*Tip*

If you use a large man's jumper, you may be able to cut the cover from one sleeve in a single piece. The sleeve cuff forms the opening edge. Position the sleeve seam at the centre back and stitch across the bottom, then simply sew on the heart and you're done!

## *Instructions*

1. Lay your hot water bottle on a piece of tracing paper and use a pencil to draw around the outline, allowing about 1.5 cm (⅝ in) extra all around.

2. Cut out your pattern.

3. Turn your jumper inside out and lay it on a flat work surface. Pin the pattern in place on the jumper, positioning the opening neck edge of the pattern on the basque (that is, the ribbed hem on the bottom edge or sleeve cuff) of the jumper. I've found that the ribbed basque works nicely for the opening, because it is stretchier and looks 'finished'.

4. Cut around the edges of your pattern, cutting through both layers of wool.

5. Cut out a heart shape from the contrasting wool fabric, using the tracing paper to make a pattern if you don't feel confident cutting it freeform.

6. Hand-stitch or machine-zigzag the heart to the right side of the centre of one of your cover pieces. (It is easier to do this before the two pieces are sewn together.)

7. Place the two cover pieces together again, right sides facing each other and simply sew around the outside edges, allowing a 1.5 cm (⅝ in) seam.

8. By hand, sew the seam allowance flat just around the rim of the opening to neaten it up.

9. Turn the cover right side out and insert your hot water bottle while it's empty, by squeezing it in half and working it through the opening. You're good to go.

# Silky nightgown case

## You will need

- Two rectangles silk or satin fabric, each 40 x 50 cm (16 x 20 in)
- 2 m (2¼ yd) narrow ribbon
- Dressmaker's scissors
- Sewing machine and thread
- Machine needle for sewing silk
- Iron
- Large safety pin

Specially-made cases for clothes, bags and shoes are a little bit luxurious, don't you think? I once stayed at the Ritz Carlton in Singapore and the famous hotel chain provided drawstring bags for everything, from laundry to toiletries, all bearing their regal blue insignia. That must be when the link to a privileged jet-set was established in my mind, because I imagine these bags will protect my favourite things as though they were wrapped in cotton wool.

This silky number saves you from folding away your bedwear in the morning – stash your crumpled pjs in here. Nightgown cases are also great for injecting new life into old silk slips that have seen better days.

Here, I've used a pale pink cheongsam that, sadly, I know I'll never fit into again, and a drawstring made of pretty ribbon that once held together a bouquet of flowers.

Make the same case in simple non-stretch cotton for a useful bag for laundering delicates in the washing machine. Simply knot the corner of the drawstring to stop dainty things escaping.

## *Instructions*

1.  With *wrong* sides together and allowing a 6 mm ($^1/_4$ in) seam, stitch your rectangles down the two long sides and across one short edge, leaving 6 cm ($2^1/_2$ in) unstitched at the top opening edge of each side seam. Tie off the threads of your seam securely.

2.  Now carefully trim this seam allowance back to 3 mm ($^1/_8$ in) and trim diagonally across the corners to reduce bulk.

3.  Turn the bag inside out, so that the right sides are facing each other and, using your iron, press the bag carefully so that the seamed edges are nice and flat.

4.  With the right sides still together, stitch a second lot of seams along the sides and across the bottom, this time allowing a 1 cm ($^3/_8$ in) seam and leaving 6 cm ($2^1/_2$ in) unstitched at the top of each side seam, exactly as before. Tie off the threads of the seam securely. (This double seam is called a French seam and it is used to completely hide any raw edges and prevent fraying, especially on delicate fabrics, such as fine linen and silk.)

5.  Turn the bag right side out and press again. On the unstitched part of the seam at the top, press under the seam allowance in the way that it wants to go, pressing it nice and flat.

6.  Now press under 1 cm ($^3/_8$ in) on the top raw edges of the opening.

7.  Press under another 2.5 cm (1 in) on these edges and stitch the hems in place close to the inner edge. You have now created a neat hem with an opening at each end. This is the casing for your ribbon.

8.  Cut your ribbon in half, into two 1 m (39 in) pieces.

9.  Attach the safety pin to one length of ribbon and thread the ribbon through the casing, guiding the pin carefully past the little fold of fabric at the edge of the casing. Take the ribbon through the casing on one edge till you get to the other end, then take it across the opening and into the remaining edge until you get back to your starting point. Knot the ends of the ribbon together or, for an even neater finish, overlap the ends of the ribbon and stitch them together with small strong stitches.

10. Repeat this process with the second length of ribbon. Pull the excess ribbon on each piece so that you have an equal loop on each side.

11. To draw up the bag, pull gently on each loop.

# Bellissima bookmarks

Sometimes it seems like there's nothing more decadent than lying in bed reading a book. Saturday mornings, weekend afternoons, early in the evening or on 'duvet day' breaks from work.

Reading, and indeed books themselves, are one of my great passions, so just the thought of books laid carelessly facing down, spines cracked or dog-eared, upsets me. A bookmark can be made of anything – a drinks coaster, a receipt, even a hairpin – but how much more stylish to make one out of leather or cloth which you'll hold onto for much longer?

Use scraps of fabric too small to do anything else with for this easy-peasy project. And if you don't feel like stitching, simply glue scraps of fabric or pretty paper onto recycled cardboard instead.

## For a Fabric Bookmark

### You will need

- Two nicely matched pieces of fabric, each about 4 x 23 cm ($1^3/_4$ x 9 in)
- Pinking shears
- Sewing machine and thread in a bright contrasting colour

### Instructions

1. Align your fabric pieces, wrong sides together.
2. Use your pinking shears to cut around the edges – this will stop them from fraying.
3. Stitch a straight line around all four edges with your contrasting thread.
4. If you're feeling particularly confident, stitching slowly on your machine, try stitching the first letter of your name or a simple image, such as a star or a circle in the middle to personalise it.

## For a Cardboard Bookmark

### You will need

- Small scraps of fabric or paper
- Cardboard
- Paper scissors
- Craft glue

### Instructions

1. Cut your cardboard to roughly 4 x 23 cm ($1^3/_4$ x 9 in).
2. Arrange your pieces of fabric or paper over the cardboard and create a collage you are happy with.
3. Glue the pieces into place.

# Soothing face pillow

## You will need

- Soft cotton fabric, approximately 30 cm (12 in) square (remember, this is going to lay across your eyes and face, so be fussy like Goldilocks and make sure it's just right. Don't use anything mixed with acrylic or delicate materials like silk or satin. You'll be heating the compress up in the oven so you don't want it singed or melted)
- 1 kg (2 lb) packet brown rice (white works just as well but I prefer the earthier smell of heated brown rice)
- ½ cup dried lavender or other dried herbs, flowers or spices you like the smell of (I've made one of these with a loose-leaf chai tea preparation and the scent was delicious)
- Sewing machine and thread
- Mixing bowl
- Needle and thread

## Instructions

1. Fold your fabric in half, right sides together, so it measures 15 x 30 cm (6 x 12 in).

2. Allowing a 1 cm ($3/8$ in) seam, stitch around two edges, leaving an opening at one end.

3. Make another line of stitching close to the first, for strength – the weight of the rice will test the seams of your fabric.

4. Finish the edges of the fabric with zigzag stitch, to prevent fraying.

5. Turn the cover right side out.

6. Combine the rice and lavender (or other spices) thoroughly in your mixing bowl.

7. Pour the contents into the opening of the pillow.

8. Turn under the seam allowance on both raw edges of the opening, then sew the edges together with a needle and thread, using small, closely spaced firm stitches, so that the rice can't leak out.

9. To use your pillow, heat the oven to 120 degrees Celsius (250 degrees F), then pop your pillow in for 5–10 minutes. Remove with mitts, allow it to cool down a little, then take it to bed. Bliss!

This is for when it all gets too much. You've had a big night, or been rocking the graveyard shift, consoling a sick child, or you plan to pamper yourself *just because*.

When I'm attending evening events for work or with friends after a long day, I always try to get home – even for an hour or so – to have a quick shower, touch up my makeup, put on a fresh frock and lie down with my feet up for 15 minutes, hot compress over my eyes (usually before I put on the fresh frock). It's amazing how much energy it gives you to keep going for another few hours. But avoid opening a bottle of red until you're home for good at night. It's murder propelling yourself back out the door after that first sip.

## Tip
The face pillow can also be used in summer – pop it in the fridge or freezer to cool you down when the weather is steamy.

## *Couch potatoes don't have busy hands*
# Curl up on the sofa

I've already waxed lyrical about how much I love hanging out on the sofa and find reasons to conduct all business from there. Essentially, I'm an energetic person trapped in a homebody's lifestyle. I say trapped, but that's my excuse for not being the kind of woman who plans many weekends away hiking, skiing or cycling anywhere further than my local farmers' market.

For me, weekends should be reserved for reading the papers, propped up in bed, being served copious cups of tea by a manservant (your partner, if they're willing). Also dinner or coffee with friends, market shopping, chatting, sewing, painting, watching DVDs, changing the house around, food shopping and cooking. You'll probably get just as much exercise fitting all this in as those 'up at 5am for a triathlon' types. I'm not opposed to getting up at 5 occasionally, but I want a good bargain to show for it. A pair of perfectly scuffed cowboy boots, say, or a vintage parasol. Is it wrong to admit this gives me the same glow of personal achievement?

When it's miserable outside, some of the above activities have to be curtailed. Ditch the shopping, order groceries online and invite friends over instead (thus cleverly avoiding stepping out in any foul weather yourself). Now's a good time to pull out all the bits and pieces you've stored up in your projects cupboard and array them around yourself on the sofa. Make sure everything is within easy reach and relax like the Queen Bee. Plan an afternoon of chatting over cross-stitching, appliqué or beading – anything you can do with needle and thread rather than a machine or messy paints and glues. (I tried putting my sewing machine on the coffee table once so I could sew and still stay perched on the sofa,

but I wouldn't recommend it. It's not very ergonomically correct, and downright silly if your coffee table's made of glass, as mine is ...)

And don't apologise for not being the outdoor type. Some of us just aren't made that way. My husband is one of those 'up at 5am for a triathlon' types, but if I accompany him on short hikes a few times a year, he lets me get away with whole weekends spent at home, doing little more than perfecting my favourite banana bread recipe.

# Funky cross-stitching

## You will need

- Blank cross-stitch fabric (called Aida from a fabric or crafts shop)
- Pencil
- Embroidery thread
- Large needle

## Instructions

1. Decide on your image and words, and draw them directly onto your blank cross-stitch fabric. This will serve as a stencil or guide for your stitching.

2. Maybe you want to go for something in a simple monochrome, but you could also think about playing with different colours for a fun look. Work out where each colour will go before you get started.

3. Thread your needle, knot the end and start filling in your stencil with stitches that look like a small 'x'. This is why they call it cross-stitching. Single stitches are fine, but then you might need to call it a tapestry ...

Cross-stitching is one of those homespun crafts that reminds me of that old TV show, *Little House on the Prairie.* I can just see the Ingalls women in their Liberty prints doing needlework by candlelight, perhaps stitching a cushion or wall plaque bearing such homey sentiments as 'Bless this House' or 'Home Sweet Home'.

Cross-stitching can be good clean family fun, but there's nothing to stop you getting cheeky with it. Think slogan t-shirts and retro kitsch. Try 'Ooh la la', 'Coffee, tea or me?' or 'Thanks a latte' with a steaming mug underneath. Or how about using an inspirational quote, like 'From little things, big things grow'? I quite like 'Better a day as a lion, than a lifetime as a lamb'. (Then again, aren't the meek meant to inherit the Earth?) Or ripping off a friend's favourite saying – 'Whatever' or 'Crazy as a Coconut' – and then surprising them by giving it to them as a gift.

You can always buy a pattern (there are tonnes to choose from, but you have to hunt hard for one that isn't too tacky and brings to mind frilly loo roll holders), so go for something personal instead. Buy a small frame to display your handiwork on the wall, or appliqué it to a cushion or carry bag.

# Embroidering bags, clothes, canvases and anything that sits still

There are so many ways to embellish your home or clothes without making them look too fussy or frou-frou. And as with any art, getting it right is often about knowing when to stop. Skill comes second to that crucial quality: imagination.

I've mentioned before my love of the French language and culture. Think about adorning plain clothes, accessories, chalkboards, canvases and even windows with a favourite phrase or simple line drawing to add whimsy or interest. Be inventive – you can always change it when you get bored or stop noticing it. 'C'est vrai!' (It's true!) stretches across the back of one of my cashmere jumpers, pockets featuring the outline of two small love hearts. Purchased on sale from a high street chain, I wanted it to look different from any others I might pass in the street. I also have a dark grey one which screams 'Zut Alors'. If Italian's more your bag, try 'Ciao bella' or 'Grazie'.

## *You will need*

- ◉ Dressmaker's chalk
- ◉ Embroidery thread
- ◉ Large needle
- ◉ Jumper, canvas, scarf, soft toy or anything, really

Ciao bella

Zut Alors

MISS OLIVE HAS ARRIVED

la vie en rose

c'est vrai!

The chalkboard in our kitchen has 'Miss Olive has arrived' scrawled across it, from the day we brought her home from the hospital. I've also drawn a picture of a bicycle with 'James is lovely' written above it, because he's a keen cyclist. I've used a graffiti texta (good for writing on glass) to pen a love poem on the window by his side of the bed, and painted numerous canvases which feature a name or single word such as 'parfait', which I have given as gifts.

Embroidering is not the only way to adorn things, but here's some quick instructions on how to do a simple chain stitch if you prefer thread to chalk, pen or paint.

## Instructions

1. Use your dressmaker's chalk to draw the outline of letters or an image on your chosen item. This will make it easier to put your embroidery in the right place. Cursive writing usually looks most effective, but experiment. You might like to toughen up a frilly white cushion with a skull and crossbones sewn in black thread.

2. Take your threaded needle and knot the thread at one end.

3. Bring the needle from the wrong side up through the fabric or canvas, at one end of your chalk design. When all your thread is pulled through, put the needle back in the same hole where it emerged in the first place, and pull the thread back through, leaving a small loop (see diagram on page 264).

4. Bring the needle back up through the top end of this loop, to create the next stitch.

5. Repeat Steps 3 and 4 to continue embroidering.

6. When you're done, sew the last loop in place a couple of times for strength, then tie a knot on the inside of the fabric.

7. Snip off any loose threads, and if you're washing the item in the machine in future, put it on a delicate wash to protect the stitches from being pulled out of shape.

# Fight off the Mean Reds with pompoms and tassels

A few years back, a friend of mine was diagnosed with breast cancer. As with any illness that strikes seemingly out of the blue, I felt sad and helpless, and couldn't find the words to comfort her. I can only imagine what she was feeling at the time, and still wince remembering that I started crying when she told me. My friend needed me to be positive for her, but ended up consoling me instead.

That night, I went home and invited over another friend we have in common. We talked about it, drank quite a lot of red wine, then spent the evening on the sofa making pompoms for a nutty rainbow necklace to cheer her up. We took photos of ourselves modelling it for an 'instruction manual', to give her an idea of how to wear it, should she be crazy enough to do so.

I don't know if my friend still has the necklace or if it even worked cheering her up for a minute or two, but it made us feel better. Doing something with our hands felt like a good way to channel our worry and our wishes for her to make a speedy recovery. You'll be pleased to hear that she is now doing well after a long course of treatment.

There's something about pompoms that makes me smile just looking at them. They remind me of times spent creating them as a child, and trips to the snow or the rugby, wearing one atop a favourite beanie – all good memories. Make pompoms to display in a bowl, for children or your cat to play with, or a single one for a brooch or to adorn a gift. Or just to have some busywork to do with your hands while watching TV – it's very soothing.

## You will need

- ◉ Wool
- ◉ Cardboard
- ◉ Scissors
- ◉ Large tapestry needle

## Instructions: Pompoms

1. Take your cardboard and cut out a shape that looks like (and is roughly the same size as) a doughnut, including the hole in the middle. Make another one exactly the same.

2. Put your two pieces of cardboard together, then take the end of your wool and tie a knot around the two pieces.

3. Unravel the wool and re-wind it around two fingers, to create a smaller ball of wool. This needs to fit through the hole in the middle of the cardboard, so keep it compact. Cut the skein of wool from the main ball.

4. Start by pushing your small ball of wool through the hole and wrapping it around the outer edge of the cardboard. Keep winding your wool around until the cardboard is fully covered.

5. When you run out of wool, there should still be a hole in the middle. Attach another length of wool to the end of the piece that you've already wound around the cardboard. Continue winding it around and through the hole – as the hole gets smaller, you might find it easier to thread the end through a tapestry needle.

6. When the hole has almost disappeared, take your scissors and start cutting through the wool at the outer edge of the doughnut. You will see the two pieces of cardboard in the middle. Use the space in between them as a guide to cut all the way around.

7. Pull apart the two pieces of cardboard slightly and use some of the wool remaining to tie a knot tightly around the wool in the middle of the doughnut shapes. Give yourself a good 10–15 cm (4–6 in) of wool trailing on either side, so you can attach your pompom to something when it's finished.

8. Remove the cardboard pieces on either side of the knot. Your pompom will spring into a ball shape. Carefully pull the wool into place or trim if it's a little lopsided, and your pompom is complete.

Tassels are even easier to make, and work well for necklaces or at the ends of scarves. They also look cute around the collar of a plain top or on the hem of a skirt, and have a certain boho charm. They can be made from recycled wool – simply unravel an old jumper or scarf, and wrap tightly around a square of cardboard to iron out the kinks.

## Instructions: Tassels

1. Cut two 10 cm (4 in) lengths of wool from your ball and put aside for later.

2. Hold your thumb and index finger several centimetres (a few inches) apart and wind the ball of wool around them until you have a small, plump amount of wool.

3. Take your first 10 cm (4 in) length of wool and thread it through the side of wool threaded around your index finger, knotting it in the middle.

4. Take the other length and tie it beneath your index finger, also in a knot.

5. Put your scissors through the side of wool threaded around your thumb, and cut in the middle. This will give you a medium-sized tassel.

## Tip

✿ If you feel all fingers and thumbs when winding a tassel on your hand, simply cut a piece of cardboard, about 10 cm (4 in) long and as wide as the finished length of your desired tassel. Wind the wool around the cardboard – the more layers, the thicker the tassel – then thread a tie piece under the wool at the top edge and tie it off. Slip the wool from the cardboard and tie a second piece around the tassel below the tie, for the neck. Cut the folds of wool at the bottom and you're done!

# Button it!
# Fun with buttons

Everyone should have a button jar or tin to dip into when they need it. If you haven't inherited or created one over the years from your own miscellaneous buttons, you can often find them in charity shops and buy the whole thing for a song. It's much less expensive than buying buttons individually at a specialist store, although sometimes a particular project such as replacing the buttons on a jacket or cardigan requires a large, matching set that you'll need to buy new. Don't discount the idea of using a different button for each hole, though – this can look quite quirky and charming, particularly on an otherwise plain item of clothing.

Changing the buttons on a tired piece can totally revive or update it. There was a trend in the '80s for garish gold-plated metal or plastic buttons on everything, but they look pretty dated nowadays. If something from this era catches your eye because it's beautifully made or in a gorgeous fabric, consider changing the buttons and snipping out the shoulder pads. For oversized dresses or jumpers, cinch them with a belt at the waist. You'll be amazed at how on-trend they seem now.

Sift through your buttons to create a 'theme'; this means setting aside buttons in complementary colours, or perhaps all the shiny ones, or buttons roughly the same size and shape as each other. Array them over clothing, small canvases or bags until you're happy with the way they look, then stitch them into place. Contrasting threads in bright colours or metallics will make them pop.

Keep your eyes open for vintage buttons made from sturdy materials such as metal, Bakelite, wood and even bone – such quality materials are hard to find these days without spending a small fortune. Source them from op shops, markets, eBay and forgotten clothes lurking at the back of parents' or grandparents' wardrobes.

# Clever scissorwork for reinventing tired jumpers

I've amassed such a huge collection of old knitted jumpers in every shade imaginable, at times they've threatened to fill an entire room. But I also use them up just as quickly for making things. At the moment, my jumpers only take up half our linen cupboard, so in the meantime, the linen's been moved to boxes under the bed where it may have to live indefinitely.

Of all the materials I like working with, wool is my favourite, but I really don't have the patience for knitting. When I show people my creations and they realise I haven't knitted them from scratch, their first question is usually 'But won't it fray?' The answer is no. Try to think of any knits (and indeed, all clothes) as fabric you can re-use. Pre-knitted wool just requires a bit more preparation before you reinvent it. There are literally tonnes of pieces languishing in shops, markets and wardrobes that will never be worn again. I hate to think of such waste, which is why I'm encouraging you to snap them up immediately for recycling projects.

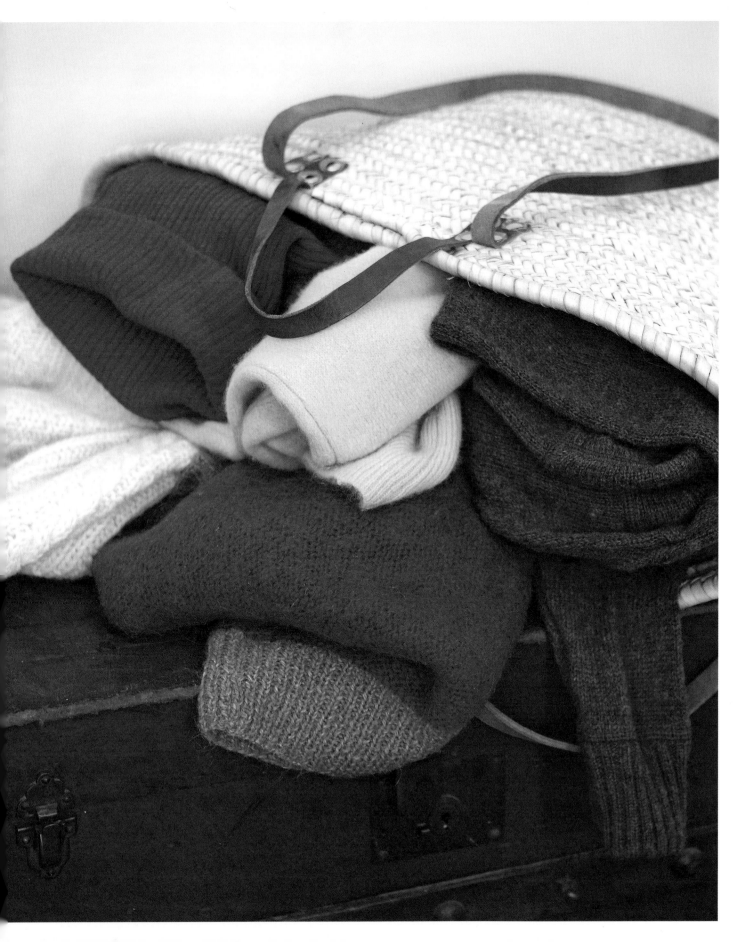

## Points to remember when you're shopping for old jumpers

◎ Buy second-hand – it's such a waste to cut up something new if you can avoid it. They will usually have some small holes or stains, which is why they've been rejected in the first place, but you can work around these.

◎ Always, always make sure they're 100% wool. Acrylic mixes tend to age badly, and never feel as good against the skin.

◎ Hunt for pure wool jumpers in both the men's and women's sections of charity shops, or at flea markets. It doesn't matter if the design is dated or ugly, because you'll be cutting them up. It's only important that you like the colour and the feel. Mohair may look gorgeous, but it's pretty scratchy up close and personal.

◎ Avoid the pieces that look and feel really thick and when you can't see the individual stitches anymore. They've usually been shrunk in the washer or dryer, and are too far gone for the following projects because what they require are the softest materials.

◎ Don't use cable-knits or jumpers with large, loopy holes as they *will* fray.

◎ Buy yourself a very good wool wash. The eucalyptus-scented variety is my favourite. If you've got a machine with a proper delicates setting, you can throw them in there once you get home.

◎ If not, don't be afraid to hand-wash. Use warm water to slightly shrink or felt fabric.

◎ If you're anxious about moths, tie your knits in a plastic bag and store in the freezer for 24 hours to kill off any eggs left in the fibres.

◎ Dry your wool in the shade laid flat on a towel and pulled into shape, then fold and store with lavender or cedar sachets for later use.

# Patchwork scarf

This is a cute and easy-to-make scarf that can be worn by a man or woman, or made into a smaller version for a child. Pick out your friend's favourite colours for a personal gift in winter. I love pink, red and white for girls or greens, greys and blues for boys, but go crazy.

## You will need

- Old jumpers in different colours but similar-feeling wool
- Scrap paper
- Pencil and ruler
- Dressmaker's scissors
- Bobble-headed pins
- Sewing machine and thread

## *Instructions*

1. Rule an accurate 10 cm (4 in) square onto scrap paper and cut it out for a pattern.

2. Line your square up against your jumper to work out roughly how many squares you can cut out from one item. Remember to line up the edge of the square either parallel with, or at right angles to, the direction of the knitted stitches. You will need approximately 54 squares in total to make a 170 cm (66 in) long scarf, but you can add or subtract if you'd like a different length.

3. Pin the pattern to your first jumper and start cutting around the outside, working your way across the jumper so you don't waste much fabric.

4. Continue cutting up your second or third jumpers in the same way.

5. When you have 54 squares, lay these down in the way they will be put together: three across and 18 down, arranged by colour. Go for a chequerboard style or random squares.

6. With right sides together and allowing 6 mm ($^1/_4$ in) seams, start sewing the pieces together, one line at a time, using the smallest stitch setting on your machine. Reverse a few times at each end of a seam for strength.

7. Zigzag the edges of each seam together for added neatness.

8. Sew the squares together into rows of three first, then sew your 18 completed rows together, one after another.

9. When you've finished sewing all the squares together, you can use the zigzag setting to stitch around the entire edge of the scarf, if you like. It's not strictly necessary but looks fantastic in a contrast thread.

*Tip*

Don't forget that as different wools will shrink at different rates, you must do all your washing and shrinking before you cut up and sew your squares.

# Poncho

## You will need

- Old jumpers in different colours but similar-feeling wool
- A largeish button
- Scrap paper
- Pencil and ruler
- Dressmaker's scissors
- Bobble-headed pins
- Sewing machine and thread

## Instructions

1. Rule an accurate 12 cm (4³/₄ in) square onto scrap paper and cut it out for a pattern.

2. Line your square up against your jumper. Work out roughly how many squares you can cut out from one item. Remember to line up the edge of the square either parallel with, or at right angles to, the direction of the knitted stitches. You will need 36 squares in total.

3. Pin the pattern to your first jumper and start cutting around the outside, working your way across so you don't waste much fabric.

4. Continue cutting up your second or third jumpers in the same way.

5. When you have 36 squares, lay these down in the way they will be put together: three across and 12 down, arranged by colour. Random squares look best for this project.

6. With right sides together and allowing 6 mm (¹/₄ in) seams, start sewing the pieces together, one line at a time, using the smallest stitch setting on your machine. Reverse a few times at each end of a seam for strength.

7. Zigzag the edges of each seam together for added neatness. Sew the squares together into rows of three first, then sew your 12 completed rows together, one after another.

8. When you've finished sewing all the squares together, fold the patchworked fabric in half crosswise, right sides together.

9. Starting at the bottom edge on one side, and keeping the squares aligned, stitch a seam along two squares, reversing a couple of times at either end for strength. This will be the centre front seam.

10. Turn the poncho the right way out, and sew your button onto the front of the opening at the top of the centre front seam. A button covered in a pretty fabric will look like a brooch when featured this way.

This is a light poncho to keep the shoulders warm, perfect for a southern hemisphere winter. The steps are very similar to the patchwork scarf, with a few small modifications.

# Boldly bright arm and leg warmers, mittens and socks

## You will need

- Sleeves from jumpers (skinnier, shrunken types work best for arms, while larger knits – men's jumpers and sloppy joes – are great for legs, but pull them on first to make sure they fit. The cuffs should still end at your wrists for the arm warmers, and ankles for the leg warmers)
- Buttons for decoration
- Embroidery needle and thread for embellishments
- Measuring tape
- Dressmaker's chalk
- Dressmaker's scissors
- Needle and thread

Although you can chop up jumper sleeves to make patches for the previous two projects, the following ideas are for using up leftover sleeves as well. Take advantage of the sewing that's already been done on the original garment, and save yourself some stitching time.

# *Instructions: Arm and Leg warmers*

1. Try on the sleeves for size. If they hang too loosely, use your tape to measure the width of your upper arms or calves, and dressmaker's chalk to mark the appropriate width. You want them to be snug, but not so snug they can't bunch up for a nice, casual look.

2. Add 1 cm ($^3$/$_8$ in) for your seam allowance. If you do cut into the sleeve, you'll need to fold the piece together again, right sides together and stitch a seam, reversing a few times at either end for strength.

3. Turn under the edge and stitch a hem at the open ends, or work around the edge a few times with a zigzag stitch in a contrasting thread for a rough, pretty look. You can also simply leave the edges unfinished.

4. For the arm warmers, unpick a small opening in the cuff end so you can pop your thumb through and the warmer can be worn like a half-mitten.

5. The arm warmers also look great with one or more buttons for decoration sewn on the hand area – bright, fabric-covered buttons work best, but any buttons will do.

## Instructions: New York mittens

1. Turn your two sleeves inside out and lay them flat.

2. Place your left hand on one sleeve, keeping all your fingers together and thumb splayed out slightly, with the cuff of the sleeve ending at the wrist.

3. Draw an outline around your hand with chalk, leaving about 3 cm ($1^1/_4$ in): 1 cm ($^3/_8$ in) for the seam allowance and 2 cm ($^7/_8$ in) for wiggle room.

4. Cut out the mitten on your traced line (through both layers of the sleeve) and use this mitten as a pattern to cut a second one from the other sleeve. (Both mittens are exactly the same at this stage, since back and front are alike.)

5. With right sides together, sew your mittens around the edges.

6. Turn the mittens right side out, then think about ways to decorate the hand area. Here I've embroidered snowflakes in white against red wool but you could put your initials, or a heart, or a simple outline of an animal.

7. Remember that once you decorate a mitten, it becomes specific to one hand, so be sure to make a mirror pair when you decorate the second mitten.

# *Instructions: House socks to make your toes wiggle*

1. Turn your jumper sleeves inside out.

2. Measure the length of your foot from mid-calf to big toe, or simply hold one sleeve against your leg and foot, with the cuff at the calf.

3. Make a mark or put a pin where your toes end, adding a couple of extra centimetres.

4. Use your scissors to chop across both sleeves at the same spot, in a straight line.

5. Sew up the open edges and turn the socks right side out.

6. Decorate with buttons if you like – *fini!*

*Adorn yourself silly*

# The Crafty Minx bejewelled

Diamonds may be a girl's best friend, but they're not too politically correct anymore, are they? As the British R&B singer Ms Dynamite sings in the track *It Takes More:* 'tell me how many Africans died for the baguettes on your Rolex?' I'm not suggesting you throw away the family jewels, rather that we consider an alternative to the bling when our natural resources are being mined into oblivion.

For this reason, it's nice to see semi-precious jewellery is back in a big way. There's nothing tacky about some of the unique, handmade jewellery made nowadays for small boutiques and luxury stores being sourced from fabric, resin, glass and all manner of organic materials. This harks back to the beginning of the last century, when Bakelite was the material *du jour* for jewellery. The revolutionary plastic is now more covetable than ever – just do a quick search on eBay to see the prices they are fetching.

Ethnic and folk-inspired embellishment is also making its biggest comeback since the '70s, with Italian design house Gucci leading the charge. The look is layers of beading and charms, mixing a variety of influences and evoking a louche, elegantly wasted charm. Fortunately, contemporary pieces are also available in local markets and street stalls all over the world for a fraction of the price; you just need an eye for separating the good from the tat.

Or make your own. Yes, home-made accessories can look a bit nutty, but that's the beauty of them. They will always grab attention, and what's to stop you passing them on as family heirlooms, no different from grandma's ruby and gold pin or sapphire engagement ring? After all, why can't a charm bracelet be made of cloth?

# Supercool biker-esque cuffs

I'm such a fan of leather cuffs. I like these because the bigger they are, the more delicate they make your arms and wrists look.

Leather is usually quite expensive to buy new, so trawl your local op shops for men's '80s bomber jackets. They will be cheap as chips, so snap them up and transform them into cuffs for you and your friends.

## You will need

- Dated leather jacket from a charity shop, for chopping up
- Pretty pieces of fabric in floral prints or bright monochrome cotton, canvas or silk (Japanese kimono fabric looks particularly fetching against tough-looking leather)
- Self-adhesive Velcro to fit width of cuff, or Velcro dots
- Dressmaker's scissors
- Sewing machine and leather sewing machine needle

## Instructions

1. Cut your leather 5 cm (2 in) wide and 17 cm (7 in) long, to fit your wrist (and then some).

2. Position the self-adhesive Velcro or Velcro dots onto the top side of the length of leather, and the underside of the other end, so that when it's wrapped around your wrist, it will fit snugly.

3. Take your pieces of fabric and play with different ways of laying them out over your leather. Leave a border so the leather is visible.

4. When you've worked out where you want your fabric to go, turn under the raw the edges of each piece and use the machine to hem around the border, to avoid any frayed edges. Remember to change the machine needle to suit the fabric, before changing it back to the leather needle for the next step.

5. Sew the fabric piece into place on the leather cuff. Make another for your right wrist, in manner of tough Iron Maiden concert-goer or owner of Harley-Davidson. Rock on.

# Ribbon brooches

## You will need

- About 50 x 3 cm (20 x 1¼ in) wide striped grosgrain ribbon
- Small swatch of fabric, about 5-cm square (2 in)
- 1 button
- Metal brooch clasp
- Bobble-headed pin
- Pinking shears
- Needle and thread

## Instructions

1. Take your small piece of fabric and cut into a circle with your pinking shears. Put it aside with your button.

2. Take your ribbon and fold one edge over to create a loop of a few centimetres (about an inch or so).

3. Use your thumb to hold down the loop, then fold the longer end of the ribbon over into another loop. Keep doing this until you have run out of ribbon, changing the angle of the loops to achieve a star-shape composed of six or eight loops.

4. Use your bobble-headed pin to hold the loops in place.

5. Grab your fabric and button, remove the pin (still holding the ribbon in place with your thumb) and place them at the star's centre.

6. Sew the button into place through all layers. You can also sew a circle around the button so the hand-stitching is visible, if you like.

7. Sew the brooch clasp on at the back. Award to your No 1 favourite friends and children.

Have you ever wondered what to do with the gorgeous ribbons wrapped around gifts or bouquets of flowers, apart from re-gifting them? I had a shoebox full of ribbons I'd been collecting for years until I started turning them into fabric jewellery. Now I have to organise entire shopping expeditions around hunting down new and interesting supplies.

Stationery shops can be a great source of ribbons and, of course, the haberdashery sections of department stores, which usually have a good range. There are tonnes of beautiful styles from around the world to be found on the web, and shops specialising in the art of *passementerie* (artfully crafted trimmings and edging). If you died and went to ribbon heaven, I have a feeling it would look something like VV Rouleaux's London store. It is a veritable cornucopia of delicious ribbons and I have spent many hours debating the merits of crisp, striped grosgrain over the lush charms of velvet and silk, and have walked out buying vast lengths of each when I only needed a metre.

These brooches look a little like the 1st place ribbons awarded at school sports carnivals and really brighten up a plain cardigan or top. They're so quick to make, you can set yourself up with a production line and make 8-10 in an hour. Put them away for easy gifts later on or use to doll up any simple bag, soft toy, hat or anything, really.

# Ribbon and fabric necklace or bracelet

## You will need

- An old strand of beads
- Approximately 1 m x 5 cm-wide (39 x 2 in) fabric, for a necklace (shorter for a bracelet) – delicate silk or organza looks most spectacular
- 0.5 m x 15 mm-wide ($^2$/$_3$ yd x $^5$/$_8$ in) ribbon
- Dressmaker's scissors
- Needle and thread

I don't think I've been to a flea market or charity store yet that didn't have a box of odd bits and pieces, with single earrings, broken brooches and old or broken strands of beads all tangled up together. What a boon for the patient hunter-gatherer! While they're usually too damaged to be worn as is, they make a good base for this reinvented necklace or bracelet. This project is so simple, there's no reason why you can't have one to match every outfit.

## Instructions

1. Cut the original string from your necklace and separate all the individual beads.
2. Take your fabric strip and tie a knot at one end.
3. Wrap the fabric around the bead, twisting and tucking the edges under, and tie another knot to secure the bead in place.
4. Repeat the previous step until you have an entire string of covered beads.
5. Cut your ribbon in half, sewing each piece to the end of the string of beads.
6. Trim the ends of the ribbon at an angle to prevent fraying.
7. Tie ribbon in a bow to secure beads around neck or wrist.

## *Wrapped to perfection*

## ... the finishing touches for gift giving

So you've created your own gorgeous gifts for friends and family. Well done! But they're not quite ready to hand over yet ... We all know how important first impressions are: wrapping most offerings is so much nicer, looks infinitely more appealing than a retailer's bag thrust hastily into the hand, and shows someone you've spent some extra care and consideration on their gift. But while it's easy to spend big on wrapping paper, you really don't need to. In the same spirit of thrifty resourcefulness, Crafty Minxes can make their own from scratch to create gifts that are precious – both inside and out.

Here are some simple ideas for best-dressed presents to knock their socks off.

# Chic and easy wrapping

I'm a sucker for brown paper packages tied up with string. I clearly watched *The Sound of Music* one too many times as a child, but Maria was right: along with warm woollen mittens, these *are* a few of my favourite things. This is wrapping at its most simple but it's very chic, regardless of what's in vogue.

*The beauty of brown paper packages tied up with string ...*

## You will need

- Roll of brown paper
- Twine
- Sticky tape
- Scissors

## Instructions

Buy twine from a newsagency or thrift store. A large ball will set you back a few dollars and last for ages. Buy a roll of brown paper. Get wrapping.

255

# Presents in threads

Another idea is to use fabric rather than paper to wrap your gifts – this is a clever way to use up small pieces of material you haven't found a use for. Pinking shears will finish it nicely with zigzagged edges. Choose calico with a brightly coloured ribbon, or patterned fabric with a simple white grosgrain or satin ribbon for a chic and timeless look.

## You will need

- Square of fabric, large enough to fit your present
- Ribbon
- Pinking shears

## Instructions

This is so easy I won't even patronise you with instructions – just fold your present into the fabric and tie a bow around it. *Fini!*

Boxes are great for small items like jewellery and keys that might get lost otherwise, and for those oddly shaped, difficult-to-wrap gifts. A beautiful box also has a much longer life than pretty paper, because it can be re-used again and again.

Find boxes from a stationery or two-dollar shop – my favourite kind is the takeaway noodle box, with its little metal bar across the top. Gold stars, origami paper and small pieces cut from old magazines can be glued to them for delicious-looking treats. Alternatively, collect old boxes from shoes, kitchen drygoods, appliances, etcetera. Cover in brightly coloured acrylic paint and stuff your present inside, cushioned by a few layers of scrunched-up tissue paper. Gorgeous!

# Boxed treats

## You will need

- Plain noodle boxes from a stationery or two-dollar shop
- Gold or silver stars
- Origami paper
- Cut-outs from magazines
- Scissors
- Glue

## Instructions

Take your box and all your decorative materials, then start going crazy with the glue until your box is completely transformed.

# Design your own paper

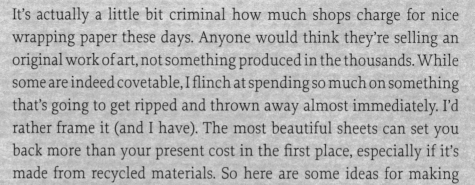

It's actually a little bit criminal how much shops charge for nice wrapping paper these days. Anyone would think they're selling an original work of art, not something produced in the thousands. While some are indeed covetable, I flinch at spending so much on something that's going to get ripped and thrown away almost immediately. I'd rather frame it (and I have). The most beautiful sheets can set you back more than your present cost in the first place, especially if it's made from recycled materials. So here are some ideas for making your own beautiful wrapping paper, or for stretching the cost of the most divine, irresistible pieces across a number of gifts.

## Collage wrapping paper

- Buy a beautiful sheet of origami paper. Cut small squares and triangles from it, then stick them to plain white butcher's paper in a pleasing layout – the dense pattern and gold or silver leaf often looks better with a bit of white space around it anyway. A plain background will make the designs sing, and your one sheet of expensive paper should take you through a few months or more of gift-giving.

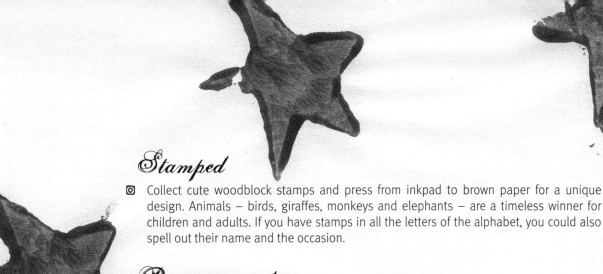

### Stamped

◎ Collect cute woodblock stamps and press from inkpad to brown paper for a unique design. Animals – birds, giraffes, monkeys and elephants – are a timeless winner for children and adults. If you have stamps in all the letters of the alphabet, you could also spell out their name and the occasion.

### Potato-printed

◎ Cut a potato in half, carve out a simple design, such as a star, with the sharp tip of the peeler, dip in a jam jar lid filled with brightly coloured paint and press onto paper. Wait for it to dry and then use to wrap your parcel.

### Newspapers

◎ Collect foreign newspapers to recycle as wrapping paper. Cover with a sheet of clear plastic – either coloured or plain – and tie a beautiful bright ribbon in an extravagant bow on top. My favourite is a Japanese or Chinese newspaper – I just love the way the ancient characters scroll down the page.

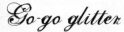

### Go-go glitter

◎ Encourage children to be creative with paint, scissors, glue and small sparkly things, such as sequins, stickers and glitter. Give them a roll of butcher's paper and let them go wild. When they're done and everything is dry, cut the resulting artwork into smaller sheets of paper for wrapping gifts.

# Fabric and paper collage cards

A card is a keepsake of time and place: it's the cherry on top. Even a swing tag with the recipient's name on it is better than nothing if you want your actions to speak louder than words.

## You will need

- ◉ Beautiful sheets of paper and card – free postcards, magazines, gift wrap and cards you have already received
- ◉ Plain card
- ◉ Paper scissors
- ◉ Paper glue

## Instructions

1. Chop up sheets of paper or cards and stick to plain card from a newsagency or craft store.

2. For simple swing-tags, buy packing cards from the newsagency (the old-fashioned kind that were once used for marking chests going by sea-freight, with a punched hole at the top) and decorate with stamps, tiny collages and the recipient's name.

# Personalised letterhead

Email (or worse, texted) invitations for important events and neglecting to say thank you are two examples of poor social etiquette. People who do this are either incredibly thoughtless or consider themselves charmingly informal. They're wrong: it's just plain impolite. What's the worst that can happen – friends will think you're too formal? It's the same as turning up to an occasion in the smartest outfit: at worst, you look out of place, but are the best-dressed person in the room, so who cares?

Create your own letterhead from favourite fonts on the computer (I have a penchant for Copperplate Gothic Light) and run through your printer on nice thick A4 parchment. Change the orientation of the page to landscape, separate into two columns and cut and paste letterhead from the first to the second for writing paper in A5-sized sheets. Cut with a guillotine or scissors once printed, and write the rest of your letter by hand.

# Pattern templates

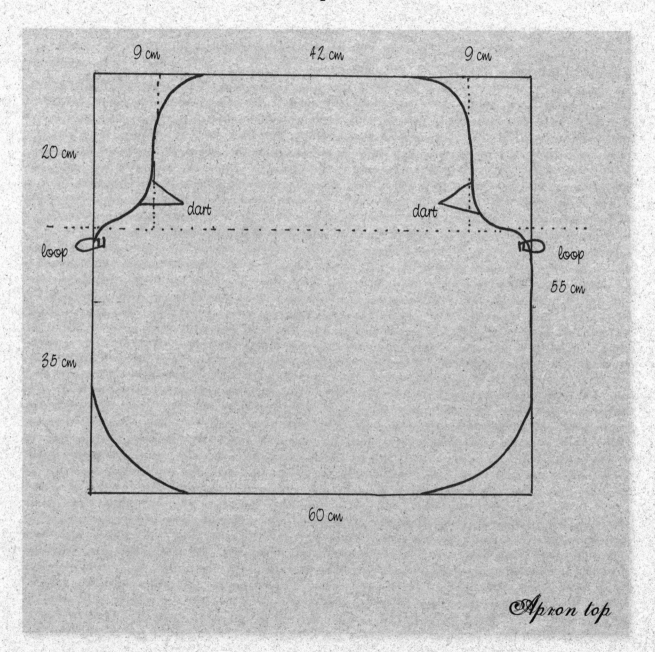

9 cm  42 cm  9 cm

20 cm

dart   dart

loop   loop

55 cm

35 cm

60 cm

*Apron top*

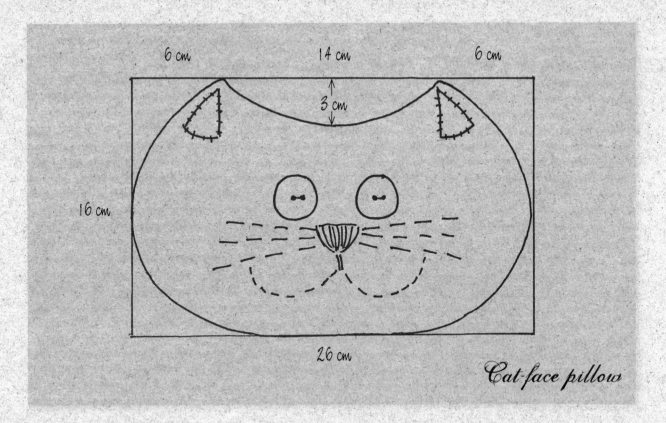

6 cm    14 cm    6 cm

3 cm

16 cm

26 cm

*Cat-face pillow*

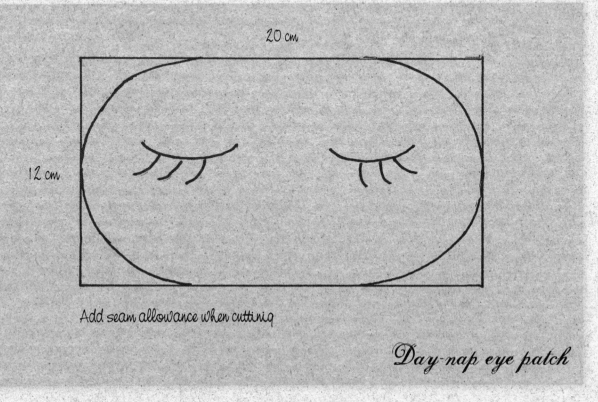

20 cm

12 cm

Add seam allowance when cutting

*Day-nap eye patch*

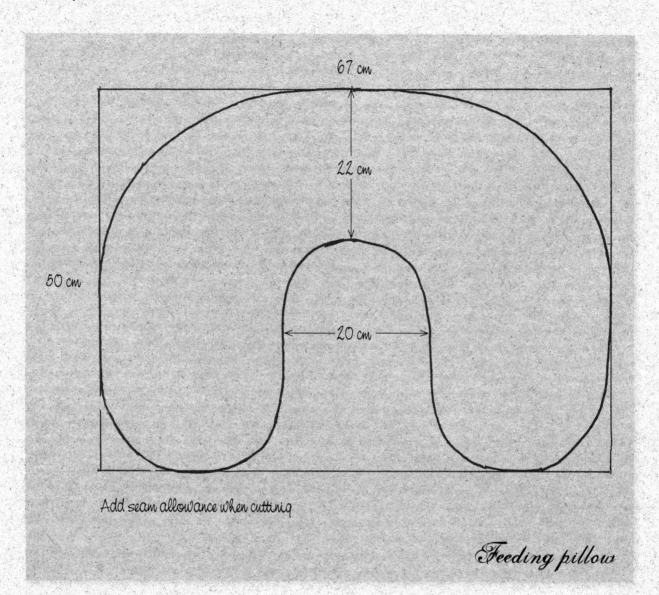

67 cm

22 cm

50 cm

20 cm

Add seam allowance when cutting

*Feeding pillow*

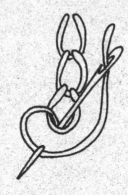

*Chain stitch*

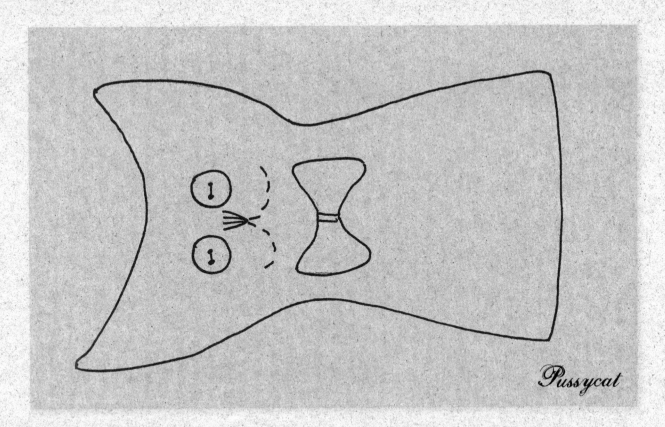

*Pussycat*

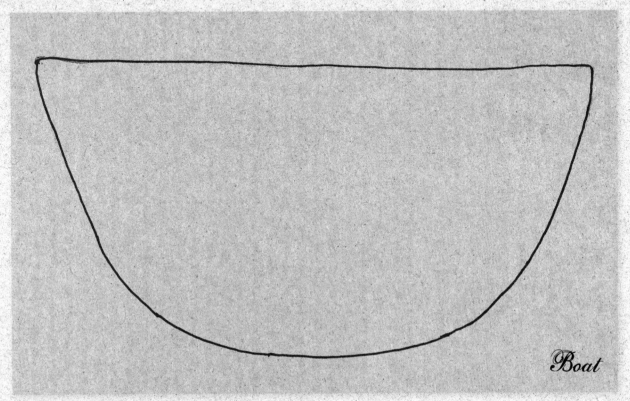

*Boat*

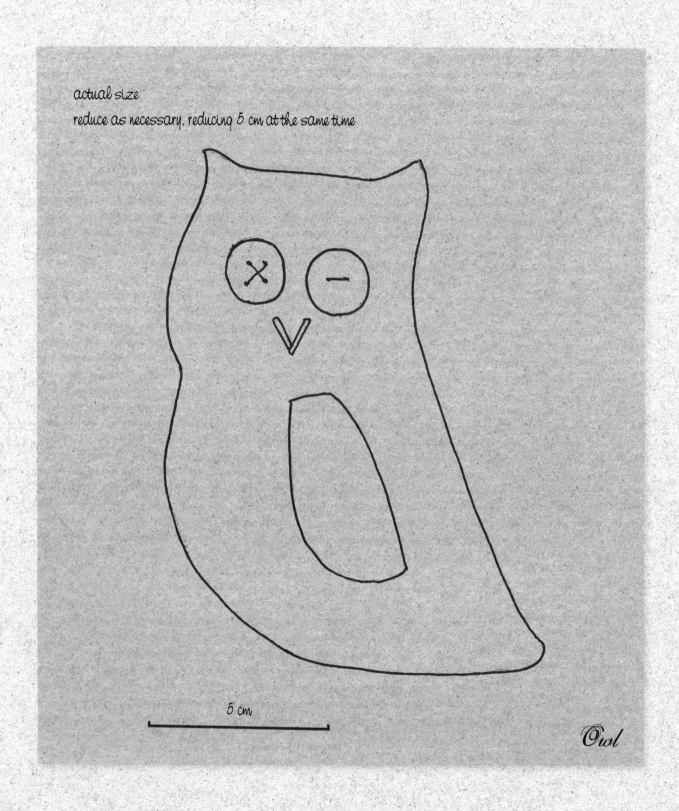

actual size

reduce as necessary, reducing 5 cm at the same time

5 cm

Owl

*Moon*

# Epilogue

In the very early stages of my pregnancy and before I even knew I was *with child*, I started writing down the instructions to some of these projects. As my belly grew so too did the idea for this book, and when I was five months along, I eventually quit my job as a book publicist to complete it, working on each season pretty much as I lived through it. You don't need to be a genius to deduce that there were plenty of biological forces at work behind my desire to write *The Crafty Minx*, which is basically a paean to nesting all year round. I finally finished writing and making all the projects shown in the book when Olive turned five months old, with a break of six weeks in between.

My point is that there is always time – and so many ways – to be creative. The last couple of years have been some of the busiest I've lived but as the saying goes; *the more you do, the more you do.* Whether you have weeks or minutes to spare, find a way to be creative when you can, because it will feed you and generate more energy than you thought possible. Ignore the undermining voices in your head. Andy Warhol became one of the most famous artists of the last century by painting tins of soup. Your own foray into creative expression could mean knitting a tricky jumper pattern, or simply penning some favourite words on a mirror in loopy cursive writing for a little inspiration. Or performing onstage in a blue latex bunny suit, *à la* Scotty the Blue Bunny. Whatever floats your boat.

Living a life that fulfils you sends out waves of karmic goodwill to everyone you come into contact with, and draws the very best things to you. Spend some time with people you love whenever possible, and be generous in every way you can. Realise that there are many different ways to show consideration, even in these uncertain economic times where spare cash is scarce. Because the clichés are true: the thought does count, and what goes around inevitably comes around. Do what you can to make the world a better, brighter place, and you'll reap the rewards tenfold. That's just the way it goes.

The karmic pleasures
of giving (and receiving)

# Acknowledgements

Of course this book would not exist without the help of a great many other people.

Thank you to my clever husband, James, who always supports and encourages me, but was especially patient and generous while I was working on *The Crafty Minx* and gave this book its title. And thank you to my gorgeous daughter, Olive, for giving me the best excuse ever to leave my job and get writing.

Thanks to my friend and former colleague, Colette Vella, who liked this book proposal from the beginning and presented it to my very talented publisher, Kay Scarlett at Murdoch Books. I feel so fortunate to have found people who got the idea straight away. Thank you, Kay – for showing such enthusiasm and commitment to this book and to me, and for championing it both internally and overseas. I couldn't think of a better home than Murdoch Books for the both of us.

And thank you to everyone else at Murdoch I have been blessed to work with:

To my editor, Sophia Oravecz, who managed the production from start to finish with skill and ease – even when she had to shave five months off the schedule overnight – and for always being kind enough to listen to my thoughts and share her own. It's such a pleasure working with you. To my copy editor, the crafts genius, Georgina Bitcon, who lay awake a number of nights thinking about how best to convert instructions from a novice into something that made sense, and for always collaborating her own ideas to make this a better book. Thank you for all your help and the cups of tea. Thank you to designer, Vivien Valk, who understood how *The Crafty Minx* needed to look even before I did and kept taking it home with her to work on over the weekend. You came up with a design much better than I could have imagined or hoped for, and always showed so much affection for these projects.

The same goes for photographers Natasha Milne and Stuart Scott, and stylist Kate Brown: thank you for giving me a book to be proud of, and for sharing your talents to convey each idea I wanted to express. Thanks to all of you for being incredibly nice and fun to work with, to boot.

Thanks in advance also go to: Mary-Jayne House, Shannon Blanchard, the Murdoch Rights and Sales teams and Murdoch Books UK for helping *The Crafty Minx* find its way to an audience.

Thank you to my former colleagues at Allen & Unwin, and to the many friends who have been so supportive of me – you know who you are. Particular thanks go to: Katrina Collett, Lisa Cosco, Guy and Corrianne Doust, John and Kristen Edmond, Carol George, Rebecca Huntley, Andrea Macnamara, Catherine Milne, April Murdoch, Anna Murray (and daughter Ruby, our model for the Tepee shoot), Clare Press (of design label Mrs Press – a number of Clare's divine pieces feature in this book), Lisa Torrance, Jacinta Tynan and Ella Walsh for their constant help, kindness and friendship.

Thank you to Shannon Fricke for your thoughtful Foreword and inspiring style, and to Julie Paterson of Cloth Fabrics for very kindly donating fabric remnants for a number of these projects. Thank you as well, Julie, for hosting my launch in your beautiful shop. Thanks also go to the talented florist, Jodi McGregor, for generously supplying her beautiful flowers for the photo shoots, and the clever ladies at Prints Charming for your divine fabrics.

And finally, the hugest thanks go to Maggie Hamilton – for her inspiration, friendship and faith in me. This book was her idea, and she not only set me the task of writing it, but also gently led me to make some monumental decisions which have made me one very contented human being. You're my fairy godmother.

Published in 2009 by Murdoch Books Pty Limited

Murdoch Books Australia
Pier 8/9
23 Hickson Road
Millers Point NSW 2000
Phone: +61 (0) 2 8220 2000
Fax: +61 (0) 2 8220 2558
www.murdochbooks.com.au

Murdoch Books UK Limited
Erico House, 6th Floor
93–99 Upper Richmond Road
Putney, London SW15 2TG
Phone: +44 (0) 20 8785 5995
Fax: +44 (0) 20 8785 5985
www.murdochbooks.co.uk

Publishing Director: Kay Scarlett
Photographers: Stuart Scott and Natasha Milne
Stylist: Kate Brown

Editor: Georgina Bitcon
Project Editor: Sophia Oravecz
Designer: Vivien Valk

National Library of Australia Cataloguing-in-Publication entry
Author:          Doust, Kelly.
Title:           The crafty minx / Kelly Doust.
ISBN:            9781741964950 (pbk.)
Subjects:        Handicraft
                 Recycled products.
Dewey Number:  745.5
A catalogue record for this book is available from the British Library.

Printed in 2009. PRINTED IN CHINA.
Reprinted 2009.